THE
GARDENER'S
YEAR

THE
GARDENER'S
YEAR

JANE COURTIER

Bath • New York • Singapore • Hong Kong • Cologne • Delhi
Melbourne • Amsterdam • Johannesburg • Auckland • Shenzhen

This edition published by Parragon in 2010

Parragon
Queen Street House
4 Queen Street
Bath
BA1 1HE, UK

Copyright © Parragon Books Ltd 2010
Design by Design Principals

ISBN: 978-1-4454-0667-1

Printed in China

NOTE
For growing and harvesting, calendar information applies only to
the Northern Hemisphere (US zones 5–9).

CONTENTS

INTRODUCTION 6

PLANT NAMES 8

EARLY SPRING 10

MID-SPRING 24

LATE SPRING 36

Tasks & plant overview 50

EARLY SUMMER 52

MIDSUMMER 66

LATE SUMMER 78

Tasks & plant overview 90

EARLY FALL 92

MID-FALL 104

LATE FALL 118

Tasks & plant overview 128

EARLY WINTER 130

MIDWINTER 138

LATE WINTER 146

Tasks & plant overview 154

GLOSSARY 156

INDEX 158

ACKNOWLEDGMENTS 160

INTRODUCTION

One of the beauties of a garden is the way it subtly alters from season to season, so slowly that sometimes you hardly notice the changes taking place. And yet the contrast between the warm and drowsy days of midsummer, with plants in full, luxuriant bloom and leaf, and the frosty midwinter, when the bare branches are rimed with ice and all plant life seems to have frozen to a halt, could hardly be more marked.

Every season in the garden has its compensations, whether it is the lusty resurgence of life in spring, the brimming bounty of summer, the brilliant colors of fall or the ethereal, sculptural beauty of plants in winter. And every season has its tasks to be performed. But while some times are far busier than others, gardening is definitely a year-round occupation if the garden is going to look good 12 months a year.

BELOW: **The pleasures of the summer garden are intensified by the gentle sound of splashing water from a garden pool.**

Perhaps one of the reasons gardeners find their hobby so relaxing is that plants won't be hurried—they need their time to grow. Although tv has made the "instant garden" seem within everyone's grasp, the reality is not quite like that. A large part of gardening's attraction stems from watching a seed or tiny cutting slowly develop into a healthy, mature plant, or watching the small, container-grown specimen you planted years ago grow into a stately, spreading tree. While it may sometimes be tempting to dream of a team of garden makers sweeping in to transform your plot overnight, how much more satisfying

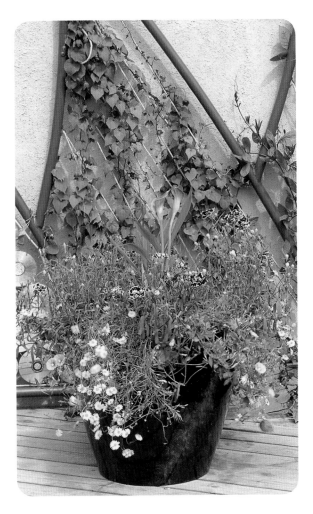

LEFT: **With a little forward planning, containers can provide color and interest for the patio virtually the whole year round.**

The gardening year divides into the four seasons of spring, summer, fall, and winter, and if these are each subdivided into early, mid and late season, we have a convenient dozen "mini seasons" to equate (roughly) with the 12 months of the year. Exactly when these fall depends not on the calendar but on the climate in your area, and local weather patterns. And that is why we use these terms rather than specific dates.

The term "ornamental garden" simply refers to the decorative, non-functional aspects of the garden—attractive flowers, trees, and shrubs.

I hope that this book will remind you of all the things you want and need to do, and also encourage and inspire you to try out some new ideas, while reminding you of all that is best in the garden in the various seasons. But most of all I hope that reading this will help you to enjoy every aspect of your garden and your gardening to the full, whatever the time of year.

it is to be able to look around with pride and say "all my own work."

People who tend gardens are usually an optimistic, forward-planning bunch—they have to be. Gardening means constantly thinking ahead. There's no point waiting until pole beans are in season before deciding it would be nice to have some of your own to pick; the seeds need sowing weeks before, in spring. And everyone knows that hyacinths make beautiful, scented houseplants for the cold days of winter, but if you want to plant your own, you have to plant them in the earliest days of fall. The problem is, of course, that because most people lead such busy lives it is all too easy to forget such things, and that is where this book comes to your aid—as an indispensable memory jogger to what needs doing and when.

ABOVE: **Freesia corms must be planted in late summer if you are to enjoy their scented blooms during the winter months.**

7

PLANT NAMES

The use of the correct botanical or scientific names for plants is always a contentious subject. Many gardeners find the scientific names unwieldy, impossible to pronounce or spell, and nowhere near as good as the common names they've been using all their lives.

Many of these criticisms are true, but there are very good reasons for using scientific names. The first is that common names are not all that common—they vary according to where you live, and often apply to more than one plant. And, of course, different countries using different languages also use different common names.

The scientific names, on the other hand, are controlled by the International Code of Nomenclature to ensure that each plant has its own unique name, and that the name denotes its family origins correctly. The names are international, being based mainly on Latin (though Greek and other languages are also used). Once the language of scientific names is understood, the names themselves can convey a great deal of information.

ABOVE: *Coleus* was originally wrongly classified; it has recently been correctly reclassified under *Plectranthus* or *Solenostemon*.

We still use the system of classification of plants developed in the 18th century by Linnaeus, who organized plants into genera and species. The botanical name of a plant is generally in two parts; the first is the genus (as in *Crocus*) and the second is the species (as in *chrysanthus*). Included in the name may be a variety (a naturally occurring, stable variation in the species) or cultivar (a variation selected or bred by man).

For greater clarity, the way the name is written follows set rules. The genus begins with an upper-case (capital) letter, the species with a lower-case letter, and both are in italics. A naturally occurring variety is also written in italics, with the abbreviation var. in front of it, while a cultivar name is written in Roman type (i.e. non italics), and enclosed in single quotation marks. We therefore have names such as *Ficus benjamina* var. *nuda*, or *Lonicera japonica* 'Aureoreticulata.'

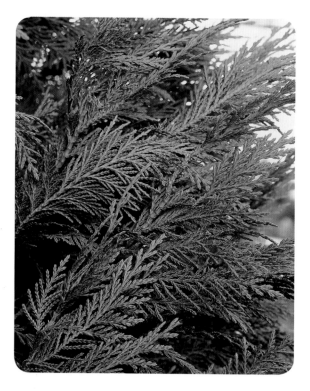

LEFT: *x Cupressocyparis leylandii*: the "x" denotes that this tree is a cross between two genera; in this case, *Cupressus* and *Chamaecyparis*.

Descriptive botanical names

alatus: winged

albus: white

alpinus: alpine

angustifolius: narrow-leaved

arachnoides: spider-like or with the appearance of a cobweb

baccifera: bearing berries

candidus: shining, white

chinensis: from China

citriodorus: lemon-scented

denticulata: toothed

dissectus: deeply cut

foetidus: having a fetid smell

fragrans: scented

glaucus: blue-gray

grandifolius: large-leaved

hispidus: spiny or bristly

laciniatus: deeply cut into narrow segments

laevigatus: smooth

lanuginosus: wooly

maculatus: spotted

maritimum: growing near the sea

meleagris: speckled

nanus: dwarf

nummularia: like coins

nutans: nodding

officinalis: having medicinal use

pictus: boldly marked, painted

procumbens: prostrate

pumilus: dwarf or small

repens: creeping

scandens: climbing or scrambling

sempervirens: evergreen

spectabilis: showy

tenax: tough, strong

tortuosus: twisted

utilis: useful

variegatus: variegated

vernalis: of spring

vulgaris: common

xanthocarpus: with yellow fruits

A hybrid (cross) between two species or genera is signified by an "x" before the name, as in x *Cupressocyparis leylandii* (a cross between two genera, *Cupressus* and *Chamaecyparis*) or *Ceanothus* x *veitchianus* (a cross between two species, in this case *C. rigidus* and *C. thyrsiflorus*).

The species names generally provide most information about a particular plant, often denoting its color, size, growing habit, flowers or place of origin. Names containing *folius* describe the leaves, and *florus* the flowers—as in *albiflorus* (white-flowered) or *cordifolius* (having heart-shaped leaves). A few common descriptive species names are given, and their meanings explained, in the box above. (Remember that the spelling will alter according to whether the genus name is masculine or feminine, following the rules of Latin grammar.)

One point that many gardeners do find annoying is the way in which the botanical names of plants are sometimes changed. These changes are not made on a whim but because new and improved techniques of plant identification have enabled botanists to discover that some plants have been incorrectly classified. *Lithospermum diffusum* has in recent years become *Lithodora diffusa*, for example, and *Coleus* has been reclassified under *Plectranthus* or *Solenostemon*. Irritating as these changes are, they are inevitable as our knowledge of the plant kingdom becomes more accurate and refined.

ABOVE: ***Lithospermum diffusum***: improved techniques of plant identification have meant that it is now known as ***Lithospermum diffusa***.

EARLY SPRING

 Ever-lengthening days give us more time to spend in the garden and we need it because there is plenty to be done. Although the days are still chilly, with overnight frost an ever-present danger, there will gradually be more sunshine to cheer things up, and a distinctly milder feel to the air.

Better weather, spring sunshine, and the obvious signs of growth and flowering around the garden make everyone feel optimistic and enthusiastic, but it pays to be cautious for a little while yet. In many places reliably warm weather is still some weeks away.

Most gardeners will be hoping for several days of dry, sunny weather, preferably accompanied by a good strong breeze: ideal conditions for drying out the soil ready for seedbed preparation. This involves raking the surface until the soil is reduced to an even texture of fine crumbs. The lighter the soil, the sooner you can start, but it's essential to wait until the soil is no longer clinging and sticky.

Although the spring may seem slow to get going, it soon moves up a gear and suddenly gardeners are hard pushed to keep up. There are spring bulbs to support and dead-head, border plants to stake before they start to flop over, containers to get ready for the summer display, and sowings to make both outdoors and inside. There's also planting and pruning to be done, and dozens of seedlings jostling for space if you have a greenhouse. In fact sometimes it's so busy that there hardly seems time

ABOVE: **There are many decorative varieties of lettuce available. The contrast of frilly-edged against plain-leaved varieties is always effective.** OPPOSITE: **The luscious purple flowers of aubrieta will brighten up any garden at this time of year.**

to enjoy the garden itself. So whatever else you do, make time to appreciate that delicious freshness of growth the garden offers now, for there's no other season quite like it.

ORNAMENTAL GARDEN
GENERAL TASKS

Increasing numbers of spring bulbs are opening their flowers every day, making a wonderful display. A little care and attention now will keep them looking good and help to build them up for next year's show. Containers will need to be planted up for summer soon, so start preparing now.

Fertilize spring-flowering bulbs

Bulbs that stay in the ground from year to year often respond well to an application of fertilizer. It does not have any effect on the current season's flowers, but it will help to build up the bulbs and ensure good flowering for the following year. Regular feeding is particularly important for bulbs which are growing in the restricted conditions of containers.

The time to feed is from the beginning of flowering until the leaves start to die down. It is recommended that you use a high-potash fertilizer, preferably in liquid form which is taken up readily by the plants. Closely follow the directions on the packet regarding volume and frequency of application.

Bulbs that are naturalized in grass are not fed very often because this tends to encourage the grass to grow strongly instead of the bulbs.

A feed can be applied every few years, however, especially if the look and performance of the bulbs is starting to deteriorate.

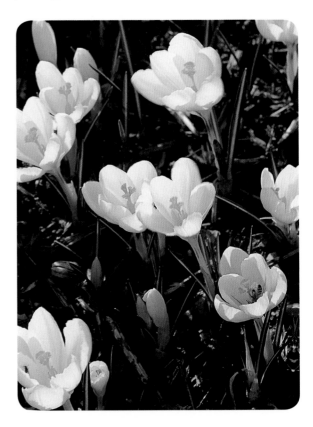

RIGHT: **An application of fertilizer while spring bulbs are flowering will help to ensure a good performance for the following year.**

Dead-head bulbs

As soon as bulb flowers fade, it pays to remove them by snapping off the stalks just below the flowerhead. This prevents the flowers from forming seeds, and directs the bulb's energy into next year's display. However, some flower stems do not snap cleanly, and the whole stem tends to pull out of the center of the bulb instead. When this happens use secateurs to cut off the heads. Note that dead-heading can only be carried out where practical, and if there are very large numbers of bulbs it becomes too time-consuming.

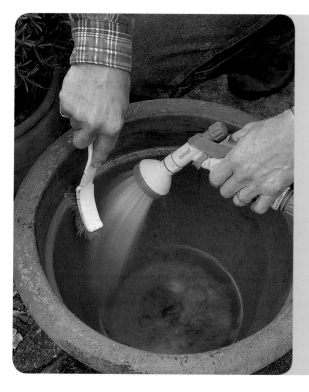

Prepare containers for summer flowers

Pots, tubs, window boxes and hanging baskets have quite likely been stored away since the end of last summer. Now's the time to get them out and check them over, cleaning them thoroughly and repairing any damage or replacing them where necessary.

Garden centers offer the best choice of new containers at this time of year because later in the spring so many people are buying them that they quickly sell out.

Containers are available in plastic, glass fiber, stone, cement, wood, ceramic, and terracotta, in a wide range of styles and prices.

If you are tempted by a particularly large or heavy container, remember to allow for the extra weight of soil and plants it will hold—some containers are almost impossible to move once they are planted up.

Mulch alpines with gravel

Most alpine plants grow well in poor, rocky, free-draining soil in cold but dry conditions. In gardens they are often killed by excessive moisture, which rots the roots, and if it gathers round the neck of the plants it can rot them at ground level.

Remove all weeds from around the plants and prick over the soil lightly with a hand fork. Then top-dress the plants with gravel or stone chippings, tucking them well under the rosettes of foliage and around the necks of the plants. This improves the drainage and makes the bed look much more attractive, which will show off the alpines to advantage.

Alpines do not have to be grown in rock gardens. A small raised bed or a shallow trough, like an old stone sink, can contain an attractive arrangement of plants and provide them with good growing conditions. Where space is really tight, shallow pans will hold individual plants or small groups, or plants can be tucked into crevices in stone walls.

RIGHT: **A fresh dressing of gravel around alpine plants helps to show the developing flowers off to perfection.**

ORNAMENTAL GARDEN
SOWING

Annual plants are among the easiest to grow, but a mixed annual border needs to be properly planned for the best results. *Lathyrus odoratus* (sweet pea), appreciated as much for its scent as its beauty, can be sown outside now, and herbaceous border plants will benefit from early staking.

Sow sweet peas outdoors

Sweet peas are often grown in rows in the vegetable garden to provide cut flowers, but they also make an attractive feature in the flower border. Dig the soil well where the sweet peas are to grow, and incorporate a dressing of general fertilizer. Tread the soil to firm it, then put the supports in place before sowing the seeds. Special cane clips are available to fix together the tops of bamboo canes making a wigwam or an A-frame, which is then covered with plastic mesh netting to give the plants something to cling on to.

Use a sharp knife to chip the seedcoat carefully to speed germination, but be careful not to damage the lighter-colored eye where the seedling will emerge. Instead of chipping, seeds can be soaked overnight in water to soften the seedcoat if preferred. Sow them about 1in/2.5cm deep and some 3in/7.5cm apart, or at the base of each cane support.

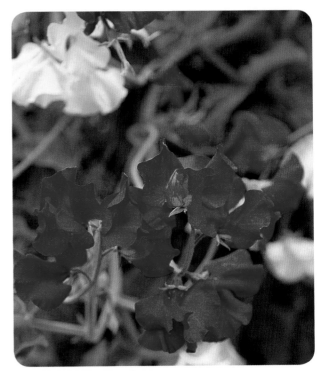

RIGHT: **Sweet peas provide wonderfully fragrant cut flowers for the home through the summer.**

Support border plants

Supports for border plants must be put in place early, well before the plants need them. In this way the stems can be trained up through the supports as they grow; eventually they will hide them totally. Proprietary supports come in various forms, which range from wire mesh rings on legs to hooked stakes that link together.

You could also use rings of canes encircled by garden twine, or twiggy sticks cut from the hedgerow. Whichever method is chosen, aim for a natural effect—unsympathetic staking, where whole plants are tightly trussed, each to a single cane, can ruin the whole effect of the herbaceous border.

Sow an annual bed

Annuals are among the easiest of flowering plants to grow, and provide many weeks of bright color in the summer. Sowing outdoors of hardy varieties can start now, as long as you choose hardy varieties. Alyssum, calendula (marigold), clarkia, *Centaurea cyanus* (cornflower), *Limnanthes douglasii* (poached-egg plant), nemophila and *Nigella damascena* are some favorites suitable for early sowing.

Hardy annuals are sown directly where they are to grow, in well-prepared, finely raked soil. Work out a sowing plan for the bed—put the tallest varieties to the back and aim for a good combination of colors and textures.

1 Mark out the sowing area for each variety by drawing a series of interlocking arcs on the bed, using a pointed stick or a trickle of sand (right). Sprinkling packets of mixed seed over the soil rarely produces a good effect.

2 Draw a series of short, parallel drills in the first patch, and sprinkle the seed thinly along the drills (left). Rake the soil over lightly and firm it with the head of the rake. Continue sowing the rest of the patches, running the drills in different directions to avoid a regimented appearance.

3 Weed seedlings will germinate freely along with the annuals, but the annuals will be easy to recognize as they will appear in straight rows. Remove the weeds regularly, and thin out the annual seedlings to their appropriate spacings when they are large enough.

RIGHT: **Colorful annuals such as nasturtiums, easily raised from seed, will always find a place among groups of mixed summer flowers.**

ORNAMENTAL GARDEN
PLANTING TREES AND SHRUBS

Container-grown trees and shrubs can be planted all year, whenever the weather is suitable. Those planted now will give an almost instant effect because they are already bursting into leaf. Herbaceous perennials are also emerging once again, having spent the winter underground.

Trees and shrubs

Trees and shrubs are particularly valuable in the garden, providing height as well as a permanent, year-round framework. There are so many different types of trees and shrubs to choose from that there is something for every garden, even the smallest plot. Shrubs can provide a range of shapes and sizes, and can be grown for their foliage, flowers, shape, or all three. Evergreens provide year-round interest, while deciduous varieties offer the pleasure of watching the leaves change with the season—unfolding in the spring, reaching their lush pinnacle in the summer and perhaps turning to glowing fall shades before falling. Flowers, too, can be had virtually all year round, even in the depths of winter when they are especially welcome.

The choice of tree needs care in a small garden because fast-growing varieties can cause problems with subsidence and damage to drains. However, there are many small and slow-growing trees suitable for small spaces including varieties of betula (birch), conifer, malus (crab apple), prunus (flowering cherry), and acer (maple).

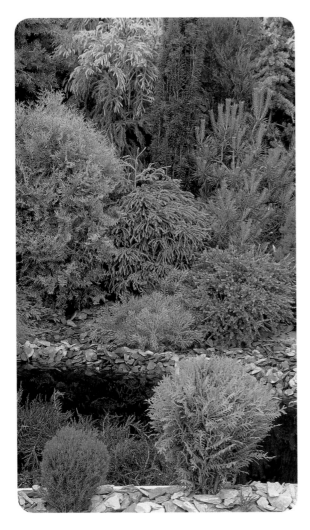

Plant herbaceous border plants

Herbaceous perennials can be planted in the fall or spring, but remember that those planted now may need watering during the late spring and early summer. This is also a suitable time to divide existing perennials that are growing too large for their position—if you didn't manage to finish all the lifting and dividing last fall it can safely be completed now.

LEFT: Evergreens provide color and interest all year. They can be planted whenever the weather is right, but now is a particularly good time.

Plant trees and shrubs

Depending on the weather, it may still be possible to plant bare-root trees and shrubs, but not for much longer. Once the dormant season is over and plants have started into growth, only container-grown specimens can be planted.

Check containerized plants sold at garden centers carefully at this time of year. Some may not be container grown, but the bare-root kind planted up at the end of the dormant season. The root ball must lift intact from the pot without the soil falling away.

A good quality container-grown plant has a firm root ball with strong, healthy roots. It can be transplanted with little check to growth at almost any time of year. Recently potted-up plants, however, will be slower to establish and may not be worth the higher cost.

Container-grown plants can be planted all year round, but spring and fall are better than midsummer when high temperatures and lack of water may put extra stress on the plant. Trees and shrubs planted now usually establish rapidly and grow away strongly.

1 Water the plant/tree well the evening before it is planted. Dig a hole deep enough for the top of the root ball to be just covered, and break up the soil at the base of the hole (above).

2 Remove the plant from its pot by tapping carefully around the edge and stand the root ball in the planting hole (above).

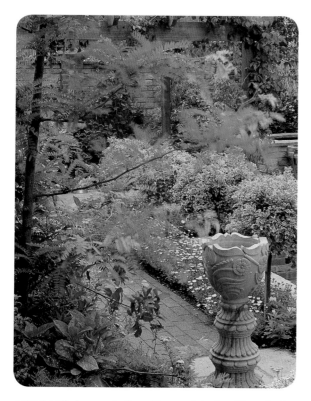

ABOVE: **A well-chosen selection of trees and shrubs adds an air of maturity and an important dimension of height to any garden.**

3 Fill in around the plant with soil, firming well (above). It is vital to keep the soil moist in the spring and summer.

ORNAMENTAL GARDEN
PRUNING

Pruning is one of those tasks that make many gardeners feel apprehensive because they know that it needs to be done, but they are not sure why or how. The main reasons for pruning are to keep the plant shapely, promote good flowering and fruiting, and encourage strong, healthy growth.

Prune roses

The first step with all types of rose is to remove all dead, dying and diseased wood. Species and old-fashioned roses (such as gallicas, bourbons, and damasks) need very little further pruning; every other year, cut two or three of the oldest stems to ground level to encourage the production of young shoots.

With large-flowered (hybrid tea) roses, all shoots should be cut back by between two-thirds and one half of their length (less vigorous varieties should be pruned hardest). Cluster-flowered (floribunda) varieties are pruned more lightly, cutting the shoots back by about one-third of their length. On both cluster-flowered and large-flowered roses, a quarter to one-third of the total stems can be cut back to the base if desired, to promote the growth of young replacement branches.

ABOVE: **Climbing plants such as clematis need regular pruning in order to promote the production of strong flowering shoots.**

ABOVE: **When pruning roses of any type, use well-sharpened secateurs to make a clean cut just above a healthy bud.**

Prune trees as necessary

Ornamental trees do not need regular pruning, but, as with all plants, any dead, diseased or dying branches should be removed as soon as they are seen; large branches could be a danger if left to fall naturally. Remove branches by first undercutting them with the saw, and then cutting from the top to sever them (undercutting prevents the branch from tearing). It is not necessary to seal the cut with pruning paint.

Prune shrubs

The correct time and technique for pruning flowering shrubs depends mainly upon the time of year that they flower. Those that flower in late summer usually flower on new wood that has been produced that season; pruning these shrubs hard now, just as they start into growth, will promote plenty of strong new shoots and provide extra flowers.

1 Shrubs such as *Buddleja davidii* benefit from being cut back severely now. Branches can be pruned to within 6–12in/15–30cm of soil level; long-arm pruners or loppers may be necessary to cut through some of the older stems.

2 Although such pruning may initially look very severe, strong new growth will be made almost straight away. Plants that are not pruned hard tend to become untidy and top heavy, with weak, straggly shoots.

3 *Cornus alba* 'Sibirica' is grown for its brightly colored winter stems, and cutting all stems back to within 3in/7.5cm of the base ensures that a good thicket of strong, bright new stems will be produced in time for next season.

4 Pruning eucalyptus back hard each spring will maintain a bushy shape and the rounded, intensely colored juvenile foliage. Cut all the previous season's stems back to within 3in/7.5cm of the main framework of branches.

5 Some shrubs that flower on older wood should not be cut down entirely in the spring, but should have about one-third of their oldest stems removed each year. This ensures that they retain a proportion of older wood to carry the flowers while new stems are produced to replace those past their best. *Cotinus coggygria* (the smoke bush), escallonia, potentilla and sambucus (elder) are among those shrubs that benefit.

KITCHEN GARDEN
GENERAL TASKS

Now is the time to use up some of those crops that have stayed all winter in the vegetable plot, and start preparing for the new season's harvest. With a little careful planning, it's possible to enjoy fresh produce from the kitchen garden at almost any time of the year.

Harvest rhubarb and kale

Rhubarb is not always considered a gourmet treat but the tender forced stems are a real delicacy at this time of year, far removed from the tough, acid, stringy stalks at the end of the season. Kale is rich in vitamins A and C, and deserves to be more widely grown. It is usually winter-hardy, grown from seeds planted in early spring and again in late summer. For an earlier crop, start seed in a tray and transplant the seedlings.

The earliest crops of rhubarb and kale are obtained by boxing up roots and forcing them into growth in a greenhouse, but plants can also be forced outdoors, covering the crowns in situ with purpose-made forcing pots or black plastic garbage cans to exclude all light.

Those covered up in early or midwinter will probably have shoots ready for harvesting now, depending on how mild the weather has been in the preceding weeks.

RIGHT: **Rhubarb is easy to grow in the vegetable garden, but it is the early, tender, forced stems that have the best flavor.**

Stake peas and beans

The peas and beans that were sown in the fall or early spring should be provided with supports as they grow. For peas this can be plastic netting, supported by stakes or canes at regular intervals; the plants will twine their tendrils around the netting as they grow. Alternatively a forest of twiggy brushwood sticks provides excellent support if you have a ready supply. Beans will also be happy with twiggy sticks, or you can provide them with a series of stakes along each side of the row, with string running around them to prevent the plants from flopping outward.

ABOVE: **A purpose-built framework to support horticultural blanket will make it easier to protect the early blossoms of fruit trees from frost.**

Protect blossom on early-flowering fruit trees

Frosts are still a distinct possibility in early spring, and will kill the blossoms on some of the early-flowering fruit trees such as apricots and peaches, often ruining the chance of a good crop. Protect trees from night frosts by draping them with lightweight horticultural blanket or, if the trees are growing against a wall or fence, attach a roll-down screen of fine-mesh netting. Make sure that the blanket or netting does not damage the blossom as it is being lowered or removed.

When fruit trees flower early in the year, while the weather is still cold, it is worth pollinating the blossom yourself in case no pollinating insects are on the wing. Use a small, soft brush to transfer pollen gently among the flowers. A cosmetic brush is easier to use than the paintbrush that is usually recommended for the job.

Use up overwintered crops

Parsnips will have remained in the vegetable garden all winter, ready for digging up and using as required. Now that spring has arrived, the roots will soon start into growth again, signaled by small green tufts emerging from the tops of the plants. As growth continues, the roots will become soft and flabby and not worth eating, and should be harvested now.

Leeks will also start into growth again, producing flower buds that develop in their second year. This results in a solid, rather tough flower stem in the center of the leek that spoils the taste and quality. Any leeks and parsnips remaining should be lifted now and moved to a spare piece of ground until they are used up.

KITCHEN GARDEN
PLANTING AND SOWING

It is time for most gardeners to start sowing in earnest at last, although gardeners with heavy soils or gardens in particularly cold, exposed positions may be better advised to hang on just a little while longer. Always garden according to the prevailing conditions rather than calendar dates.

Prepare the soil for sowing

Soil in a seedbed should be broken down to fine, even crumbs, usually known as "a fine tilth." If the soil is left in large clods it is very difficult to get a level seedbed, and seeds will end up being buried either too deeply or too shallowly to achieve good germination.

If the vegetable garden has been left roughly dug over the winter, frosts will have got at the clods of soil, breaking them up by the action of repeated freezing and thawing.

As soon as some dry, breezy weather has dried out the soil surface sufficiently, these clods can be reduced to fine crumbs by raking. Any particularly large clods can be broken down by a smart blow with the back of the rake.

Begin sowing vegetable crops

Some time during this period, depending on the weather, a wide range of vegetables can be sown, including beans, carrots, leeks, lettuces, parsnips, summer and fall cabbages, early summer cauliflowers, spinach, and Swiss chard. Draw straight drills using a garden line and a Dutch hoe, and sow the seeds thinly along the drill. Rake the soil carefully over the seeds, tamp it down lightly and label the row clearly.

It is too early for the more tender crops such as zucchini, marrows, and bush and pole beans to be sown outside, but they can be raised in pots in a greenhouse for planting out after the last frost.

ABOVE: **A light touch with the rake is necessary in order to produce a fine, even surface to a seedbed. Large stones should be removed.**

RIGHT: **Most gardens have room for some soft fruit. Early spring is a good time to plant container-grown bushes and canes.**

Plant potatoes

If growing space is limited, plant early potatoes rather than main crops, choosing some of the more uncommon varieties that are impossible to buy from the greengrocer. The earliest crops of new potatoes have an incomparable flavor when they are freshly lifted. The foliage of potatoes is sensitive to frost, so take care about the planting time. It generally takes two or three weeks before the shoots show through the soil after planting.

1 As an alternative to immediate planting, seed potatoes can be set on a cool, light windowsill to produce shoots (right). The eyes that produce the shoots are clustered together at one end of the tuber (the "rose" end), and tubers should be set in egg cartons with this end uppermost.

2 Potatoes should be planted in well-prepared soil, in rows 18in/45cm apart, and spaced roughly 12–18in/30–45cm apart within the row (below). Sprouted (or "chitted") tubers will appear through the soil more quickly after planting, but they need to be handled carefully when planting in order to avoid knocking the shoots off.

3 Draw wide drills using a draw hoe, or use a trowel to make individual planting holes. Plant the potatoes around 5in/13cm deep. Chitted tubers should be dropped carefully into the holes with the shoots at the top; these shoots are very fragile and are easily broken. Unsprouted tubers should be planted with the rose end facing up.

4 Check the rows of potatoes regularly to see when the first shoots appear; they are dark bluish-green (above). Be on your guard against frost. If an unexpected frost kills the first shoots all is not lost— new shoots should replace them.

MID-SPRING

The garden really is looking good now, with the trees clothed in fresh young leaves, lawns becoming a richer green and spring flowers at their peak. A little warm, sunny weather brings out a real enthusiasm for gardening and there's certainly plenty to keep the keenest gardener occupied.

Gardeners are not the only ones who are enjoying the spring weather, and pests and weeds are now thriving. Weeding is a job that needs to be done for a large proportion of the year, but weeds are probably growing most rapidly in mid-spring. It's especially important to keep them under control while garden plants are small because they can easily be smothered by weed growth.

Pests, too, are on the increase, attracted by the tender young growth the plants are making. Slugs and snails are often a particular problem, and aphids (greenfly) can be found clustered on shoot tips. Early action helps to prevent an outbreak turning into an epidemic.

There may be some slightly tender plants that appear to have been killed by the winter cold, but don't consign them to the compost pile. It is sometimes well into the summer before they show signs of recovery and start to put out buds. Check by gently scraping a little patch of bark from the main stem—if the wood underneath is green and moist, the plant is still alive.

Spring bulbs continue to make a stunning show; wherever possible they should be dead-headed as they fade,

ABOVE: **Most euphorbias brighten spring with their lime-green flowerheads, but the steely blue leaves often persist right through the winter, too.** OPPOSITE: **Tulips and forget-me-nots make a classic combination in the spring garden.**

before they have a chance to set seed. Spring bedding plants are also putting on a good performance; make a note to obtain more seeds of plants and buy them when you buy summer bedding plants from the garden center.

There's plenty to do in the kitchen garden, too, with weeding, sowing, and planting out, plus thinning out of crops that have been sown earlier.

ORNAMENTAL GARDEN
PLANTING AND SOWING

Alpines establish rapidly in mid-spring. If possible, grow them in a raised area so that their small but often exquisite flowers can be appreciated more easily. *Galanthus* (snowdrops) are best planted now before the leaves die down, and there are many summer-flowering bulbs to plant, too.

Plant snowdrops

Unlike many other bulbs, snowdrops are best planted while they are still in leafy growth; the dormant bulbs do not establish so well and can be disappointing. Many mail order nurseries specializing in small bulbs advertise snowdrops "in the green," and this is the best way of obtaining some of the more unusual and expensive species and varieties.

If you already have clumps of snowdrops in the garden which you would like to increase, this is a good time to split them up and replant them in new positions. Lift the clumps carefully with a hand fork and tease them apart gently into two or three smaller groups. Replant them straight away, so that they do not dry out.

Do not set the small bulbs too deep—aim for 3in/7.5cm. Heavy soils should have a little sharp sand or grit, and well-rotted compost worked in before planting.

RIGHT: **The double snowdrop *galanthus* "Flore Pleno" is a popular variety, with delicate blooms like frilly petticoats.**

Plant alpines

Alpine plants come into their own next month, and this is a good time to plant new specimens. Container-grown plants from garden centers can be bought and planted when they are coming into flower, making choosing attractive varieties easier.

Prepare the soil well, remembering that alpines need free-draining conditions. Plant with a trowel and firm in well. Dress around the plants with a little grit to ensure good drainage round the necks and help avoid the risk of rotting.

Plant summer-flowering bulbs

Although spring is the first season that comes to mind when anybody mentions flowering bulbs, there are lots of species and varieties that make a great show in the summer. They are not difficult to grow, and it's well worth planting some now.

1 Most summer-flowering bulbs like a warm, sheltered position in full sun. The soil must be free-draining to avoid the bulbs rotting; on soils that tend to be heavy, add coarse sand or grit to the planting site and fork it in well (left).

2 Bulbs should be planted as soon as they are available from garden centers. Always choose those that are large, firm and unblemished (right); avoid small and shrivelled bulbs because they will not give very good results.

3 Dig a planting hole with a trowel, sprinkle a little sand in the base and put in the bulb (left). The ideal planting depth will vary from species to species and depends on the size of the bulb. In general plant the bulb at a depth twice that of its height.

4 Cover the bulb with soil and firm it in position lightly. Once planting is completed, it is a good idea to label the planting areas clearly. This should help you to avoid accidentally disturbing the bulbs before they start to show through the soil.

LEFT: **Sunny yellow lilies are perfect for brightening up the flower borders in summer and can be planted at this time.**

27

ORNAMENTAL GARDEN
PLANTING AND PROTECTION

Every garden should have its full complement of evergreen plants. For many species this is a good time to plant, and there is a fine selection of flowering and foliage shrubs and trees to choose from. Apart from their ornamental value, they are excellent for providing shelter in a garden.

Make the most of evergreens

Evergreens are important plants in any garden, giving it form and structure which persists throughout the year. They are especially valuable in winter when other plants are bare and leafless, but they also have a role to play in the spring and summer, forming a perfect backdrop for brightly colored flowers.

Many evergreens such as escallonia, choisya (Mexican orange blossom), osmanthus, and ceanothus are a little on the tender side and are generally prone to damage from cold and wind, making mid-spring a better time for planting than the dormant season. Choose a free-draining soil and a reasonably sheltered site.

BELOW: **Evergreen hedges are both decorative and functional, especially when neatly and attractively trimmed.**

Evergreens as windbreaks

A hedge usually makes a much better windbreak than a solid screen such as a wall or panel fence because it is permeable, and it filters the wind rather than forcing it over and down in a potentially damaging blast. Evergreen hedges provide good wind protection all year round. The hedge can be formal, requiring more frequent clipping, or informal, as suits the garden style. Suitable evergreens include:

FORMAL HEDGES
Ilex (holly): many varieties, some brightly variegated and bearing berries
Ligustrum ovalifolium (privet): very common; the golden variety is more colorful
Prunus laurocerasus (cherry laurel): large, glossy, deep-green leaves

INFORMAL HEDGES
Berberis stenophylla (barberry): smothered in arching sprays of deep-yellow flowers in spring
Escallonia macarantha and hybrids: small, glossy leaves and pink or red, tubular flowers in early summer; rather tender
Pyracantha rogersiana (firethorn); light-green leaves, a froth of white flowers in spring followed by colorful berries.

Plant evergreens

Bare-root deciduous shrubs should be planted in the dormant season, but mid-spring is the best time to plant evergreens. As the weather is often dry at this time of year, special care must be taken not to let the plants dry out in the weeks following planting.

1 Prepare the planting site by digging it over deeply and adding some well-rotted organic matter such as garden compost or manure, or working in a proprietary planting mix.

2 Dig the planting hole, making sure it is deep enough for the top of the root ball to be just level with the soil surface. Break up the soil at the base of the planting hole.

3 Evergreens are sometimes supplied as root balled specimens, with the roots wrapped in netting or hessian. Place the complete root ball in the planting hole before untying and removing the wrapping material (right), then fill in with soil and firm in the plant as usual.

4 Evergreens are particularly prone to wind damage because they have their full complement of leaves at planting time. Wind strips moisture from the leaves, leading to scorching and leaf drop. Protect plants in exposed conditions by erecting a temporary windbreak (above).

5 Water the newly planted shrub thoroughly (above). Further watering will be necessary throughout the spring and summer after planting unless the weather is particularly wet; it is very important that the soil does not dry out before the plant has a chance to get properly established.

ORNAMENTAL GARDEN
PLANT PROTECTION

Much of a gardener's time is spent protecting plants from various pests and diseases, particularly in spring. Slugs are a major problem, but there are various environmentally friendly methods to deal with them. Roses need regular treatment against diseases, and the battle against weeds goes on.

Take safe action against slugs

Slugs and snails are voracious feeders on plant growth, and can do an enormous amount of damage. Slug pellets contain metaldehyde, an effective but indiscriminate poison that is also toxic to wild animals and household pets. Consequently, many gardeners have reservations about its use.

One alternative is trapping. Set shallow dishes containing beer or another bait into the soil to attract and drown slugs (though the rims must be high enough to prevent beneficial beetles from suffering the same fate), or place grapefruit or orange halves cut-side down on the soil to attract slugs that must be disposed of the following morning. Aluminum sulfate is also sometimes effective.

Biological control is a relatively new technique that is very promising; it uses a nematode with the tongue-twisting name of *Phasmarhabditis hermaphrodita*. The soil must be reasonably warm for it to work, but it can be used from now on through the summer.

Check roses for disease

Roses are subject to a common trio of diseases—blackspot, mildew, and rust. Blackspot is easily recognized because black spots or blotches with an irregular outline cover the foliage, which falls early. Mildew leaves a white powder on young leaves, stunting growth, distorting flowers and spoiling the plant's appearance. Rust is not so obvious at first; small, orange, spore-filled pustules form on the undersides of the leaves, with a pale yellow patch on the top surface. Leaves fall prematurely and the disease can severely weaken the plant.

Check the leaves regularly, including the undersides, for signs of disease. At the first sign, or even before if you have had disease problems previously, begin a regular spraying program. Several appropriate fungicides are on the market, and their use should be alternated for the best results.

LEFT: **Slugs usually feed under cover of darkness, and can quickly reduce lush foliage to a skeleton of veins overnight, especially in damp weather.**

Keep weeds under control

At this time of year everything in the garden is growing strongly, especially the weeds. Controlling them is important, not only because they make the garden look untidy but because weeds deprive cultivated plants of moisture, nutrients and light.

1 Weeds are best dealt with while they are still small, when hoeing is very effective (left). Choose a dry, blowy day so that the weeds wilt and die quickly. Run the well-sharpened blade of the hoe flat along the soil surface, slicing the seedling weeds off from their roots rather than digging them up. Hoeing is not practical where weeds are growing close to or among cultivated plants because there is too much risk of damage. Hand weeding is often the only option using a hand fork to remove deep-rooted weeds.

2 Chemical weedkillers are often very effective (left). Contact herbicides (such as paraquat) kill the top-growth onto which they are sprayed, but not the roots. They are suitable for young annual weeds but are not so effective on deep-rooted weeds that will regrow.

3 Translocated herbicides (such as glyphosate) are carried to all parts of the plant including the roots, and are best for difficult weeds such as bindweed and couch grass. Care must be taken to keep accidental splashes of these weedkillers off cultivated plants.

4 Once the soil surface is clear, apply a thick mulch of shredded bark or a similar material (below). This helps keep the ground weed free by preventing the germination of any weed seeds present in the top layer of soil. Any weeds that do appear in the mulch are easy to pull out of the loose material.

ABOVE: **A hand fork is useful to help prise deep-rooted weeds out of the soil. Regrowth often occurs from portions of root left behind.**

LAWNS
GENERAL TASKS

The lawn is an integral part of the garden, providing a restful green backdrop against which to admire the vibrant colors of the flowers. Lawns that may have looked tired and thin after the stress of the winter should now be growing more strongly, and it's time to help them reach perfection.

Apply lawn fertilizer

In spring, a fertilizer containing high levels of nitrogen will boost growth and help the grass to develop a rich green color. The phosphates and potash also included in lawn fertilizers stimulate root growth and improve resistance to disease and adverse weather conditions.

Fertilizers are available as powders, granules or liquids. Liquid fertilizers can be applied with a hose-end dilutor; they are fast-acting and give a rapid response, but they can be expensive for large lawns. Dry fertilizers can be applied by hand but it is very difficult to achieve an even distribution, and the result can be patchy. The best method is to use a fertilizer distributor, a small hopper on wheels that applies the fertilizer at a given rate when pushed up and down the lawn. Take care to cover all the grass evenly, and do not overlap strips or leave a gap between them because this will show up as differently colored growth later on.

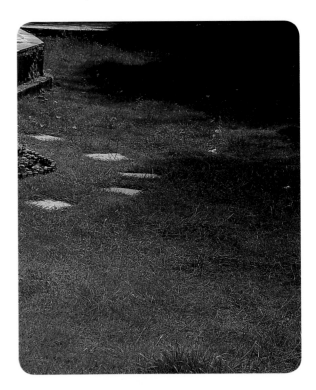

RIGHT: **Mid-spring is an ideal time to make a new lawn from seed. Sow in soil that has been carefully prepared to create a fine tilth.**

Control lawn weeds

Where there are only a few isolated weeds in the lawn they can be treated individually, either by digging them out with a narrow-bladed trowel or special lawn-weeding tool, or by giving them individual doses of weedkiller. "Spot" weedkillers come in the form of wax sticks, impregnated sponges, aerosols and ready-to-use sprays. If weeds are more widespread over the lawn surface, an overall application of selective weedkiller is necessary. This should be applied shortly after fertilizing, or you can use a proprietary "weed and feed" product that applies the two together. Be very careful not to allow lawn weedkillers to drift onto cultivated plants or neighboring gardens. Tiny amounts carried on the breeze are enough to do a great deal of damage to other plants.

Mow and edge lawns

A perfect, velvet-textured, emerald-green lawn is the envy of all who see it, but many gardeners seem to find it impossible to achieve. Understanding and employing the correct mowing technique is one simple way to improve greatly the quality of the turf.

1 Now that the grass has started to grow rapidly it will need cutting more frequently—once a week at least, and twice a week as spring moves into summer. Before mowing, clear stones, fir cones and other debris from the lawn. If you can, wait until the dew has dried.

2 Set the blades at the right height (below); scalping is a very common mistake. At this time of year the grass should be left between ¾in/18mm and 1¼in/30mm/high, reducing to a minimum of ½in/12mm high in summer (¾in/18mm is better for most lawns).

3 Mow the grass in parallel strips up and down the lawn (right). If the mower has a rear roller it will produce the light and dark stripes favored by many people; in this case it is important to keep the mowing strips as straight and even as possible for the best effect.

4 Next time the lawn is mown, work at right angles to the last direction of cut—across the lawn rather than up and down. Alternating the direction at each cut makes sure that the surface of the lawn remains even, and helps control lawn weeds and weed grasses.

5 Once the mowing is finished, trim the edges to make the lawn neat. Use long-handled edging shears or a powered edger. If the edges are ragged after the winter, recut them in spring with a half-moon edging iron (below); use a plank as a straight edge.

ABOVE: **Grass seed should germinate rapidly in warm, moist spring weather. This is a good time to repair worn patches by oversowing them.**

KITCHEN GARDEN
PLANTING AND SOWING

Time vegetable sowings so that you have a steady harvest through the summer, without a glut of crops maturing simultaneously. Be particularly careful with vegetables that have a short period of use before they spoil, such as lettuces, which run to seed, and peas, which become tough.

Continue sowing vegetables

As the weather becomes warmer, more and more vegetable crops can be sown. Among those that can be sown outdoors directly where they are to grow are beets, Swiss chard, various beans, carrot, kohlrabi, lettuce, pea, radish, scallion, salsify, scorzonera, spinach, and turnip. When you sow the crops, spacing can be varied according to the size of plant that is required.

Some vegetables are sown now in a seedbed and transplanted to their cropping positions later. They include broccoli, Brussels sprouts, calabrese, cauliflowers, summer, fall and winter cabbages, kale, and leeks.

BELOW: **Try to keep the vegetable garden weed-free. Supply supports to plants that need them at an early stage of growth for the best results.**

Sow crops for succession

"Little and often" is a good idea when it comes to sowing many vegetables for home use. This ensures that crops can be picked and used when they are young and tender, and there will be a further supply following from a later sowing. Crops that can be grown in succession include beets, cabbage, carrot, cauliflower, lettuce, pea, radish, spinach and turnip. Sow short rows of the crops in question at two to four-week intervals, or select a range of different varieties to mature at different times throughout the season.

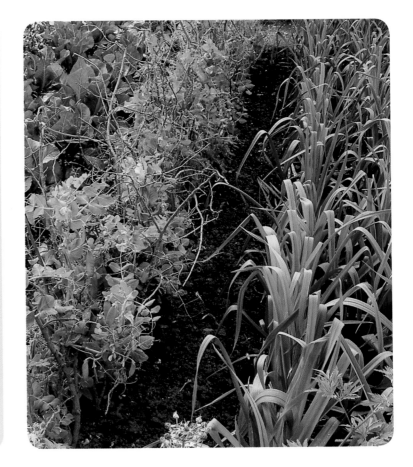

Plant onion sets

Onions are easy to grow from sets (small, immature bulbs). It is best to buy heat-treated sets because they are less likely to run to flower prematurely than those that are untreated.

1 Onions need an open position in fertile, well-worked soil which has been broken down to fine crumbs (right). Work a little general fertilizer into the soil immediately before planting.

2 The sets can be planted in drills made deep enough for the tops of the bulbs to be just showing above soil level when planted. Space them 2–4in/5–10cm apart in rows 10in/25cm apart: the wider spacing will produce larger bulbs.

3 In fine, very light soil, drills are not necessary—the sets can simply be pushed into the ground at the correct spacing (right). On heavier soil, however, this compresses the soil at the base of the set, making it difficult for the roots to penetrate; the onion sets then push out of the ground as the roots start to grow.

4 Birds are often a nuisance, tugging the freshly planted sets out of the ground. One way to avoid this is to trim away the dead, brown leaves at the tip of the set with scissors or secateurs before planting (below): these dead leaves form a convenient "handle" by which birds can tweak the sets out of the soil.

5 Water the sets shortly after planting if the weather turns dry, and keep them free of competition from weeds. Heat-treated sets are often a little slower than untreated sets to start into growth, but they soon catch up.

ABOVE: It is possible to obtain a satisfying crop of perfect, golden-skinned onions from sets planted in the vegetable garden in mid-spring.

LATE SPRING

 The weather is mild and there's often a good deal of sunshine. Spring blossom mingles with the early blooms of summer, and foliage still has a wonderful freshness. Gardeners should enjoy the last weeks of spring while they prepare for summer in what is always one of the year's busiest times.

In most areas the risk of damaging night frosts will be over toward the end of late spring but in the early days, and in colder regions, you will need to remain on your guard. If your garden happens to be in a frost pocket, you may need to be much more cautious than neighbors only a short distance away who are in a more favored position.

This is a good time to plant up hanging baskets, window boxes and tubs which are very valuable for injecting concentrated splashes of color in the garden and around the house. They are increasingly popular, with a wide range of new and unusual "patio plants" available at garden centers. Keep them under cover or in a sheltered position for a few days after planting to initially keep them protected. Spring bedding plants are past their best now, and need to be cleared out to make way for the summer bedding—but don't forget to sow spring bedding plants for next year's display.

Plants are growing strongly now but need to be regularly fed and weeded; pests must be controlled promptly. In the vegetable garden, tender crops such as pole beans, bush beans, and zucchini can be sown safely out of doors.

ABOVE: **The glossy, aromatic leaves of *Choisya ternata* (Mexican orange blossom) are a bright lime-green in the variety "Sundance."**
OPPOSITE: **The fragrant flowers of wisteria are often among the most spectacular blooms in the garden in the late spring.**

Finally, a pond is a great addition to any garden, adding a special sort of tranquillity with its shimmering water and colorful plants. This is the best time of year to build a garden pool, and you can rest assured that you are creating a feature that is bound to be enjoyed for many years to come.

ORNAMENTAL GARDEN
GENERAL TASKS

Hardy annuals sown earlier will now be making good headway, and perennial border plants need some attention to keep them in good shape. If you want to propagate garden shrubs, layering is often successful where other methods fail. Pests continue to increase in numbers around this time.

Check plants for pests

Garden pests of all sorts continue to thrive in the warmer weather, and plants need to be checked regularly and pest infestations treated promptly. One of the most troublesome pests is vine weevil. Greenhouse plants are most at risk, but the adult weevils spread outside as the weather becomes warmer. Outdoor weevil activity starts now, and peaks between early summer and mid-fall. You may see leaves that have had characteristic notches bitten out of their margins by the adult weevils but it is the damage done by the grubs that is more serious: they feed on the roots and can completely destroy the root system.

Suspect vine weevil grubs where plants suddenly wilt and die for no apparent reason, especially plants in containers or pots.

A biological control containing nematodes can be applied now, provided there is a reasonably warm spell of weather. This will be effective against larvae that emerged from eggs laid last fall.

RIGHT: **Grubs of the vine weevil eat away at a plant's root system until it can no longer support the top growth and the whole plant collapses.**

Staking border plants

Continue to provide supports for border plants from an early stage (see page 14). As the shoots grow, train them gently to the support; tie in where necessary with soft twine, plastic-covered twist ties or raffia. Where twiggy sticks are used, the border plants should be making sufficient growth to cover them almost completely. Do not allow stems to flop before putting supports in, or they will stay kinked.

This type of support can be raised as the plant grows, but great care is necessary to avoid snapping the stems.

Stakes that link together can be arranged in patterns to provide support for almost any size and shape of plant.

Taller plants such as delphiniums are likely to need individual stakes for the flowering stems.

Increase shrubs by layering

This is a simple way of propagating shrubs with low branches. Many shrubs are suitable for propagation by layering, including rhododendrons and magnolias, which are otherwise difficult to increase. Select a suitable low-growing branch that can be bent down to soil level. It should be a healthy, strong-growing shoot of the previous season's growth.

1 Bend the shoot down to the ground and mark the position where the stem touches the soil, about 9–12in/23–30cm behind the tip of the shoot (right). Dig this area over well with a trowel, then dig a hole about 4in/10cm deep with a straight, flat side farthest from the plant.

2 Bend the shoot down again to check the position of the hole. When the stem is lying at the base of the hole, the top 9in/23cm of the shoot should stick out of the ground, held upright by the straight side. Strip the leaves and leaf stalks from the length of stem to be buried.

3 Where the stem must be bent to pull it down into the hole, make a small cut on its underside with a sharp knife (right). This injury to the plant will encourage growth.

4 Peg the stem into the hole with a piece of bent wire (below), return the soil to bury the stem completely. Tread the soil gently but firmly to firm it back down.

5 Tie the protruding tip of the shoot to a cane in order to keep it upright and then water the soil regularly to keep it moist. Roots will form on the buried portion of stem over the summer, and once the layer is well rooted it can be dug up and separated from the parent.

ABOVE: **Give hardy annual seedlings room to develop by thinning them out. Select the strongest seedlings to remain at the appropriate spacing.**

ORNAMENTAL GARDEN
PLANTING AND SOWING

Most gardeners aim for a good display of flowers for as many months as possible, and now that spring bedding is past its best it's time to set out the summer-flowering plants and containers for the patio. Think a little farther ahead to providing color for the fall and winter, too.

Replace spring plants with summer bedding

In most areas spring bedding plants will have passed their best. Toward the end of this period the weather should be warm enough to plant out summer bedding to replace them, but make sure the plants have been hardened off sufficiently to survive.

Fork over the soil, removing weeds along with the old plants, and work a sprinkling of general fertilizer into the surface. Turn the new plants out of their trays and disentangle the roots: bedding plants grown in individual cells establish more quickly because the amount of root damage is reduced. Plant with a trowel, firming in well, and water in the plants as each section of the bed is completed.

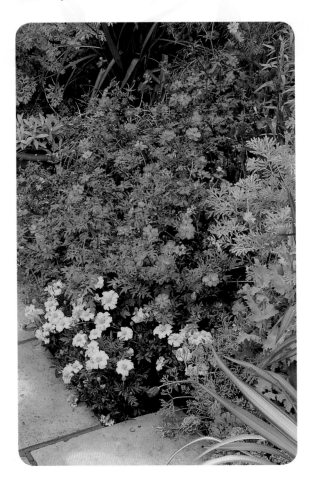

Planning ahead

Dahlias provide wonderfully colorful blooms in late summer and early fall, and now is the time to plant the overwintered tubers, or cuttings rooted from them earlier in the spring. Since cuttings should be hardened off properly, and must not be planted out until all risk of frost is over, in some particularly cold areas it will be necessary to wait a little while longer.

Flowers are at a premium in the winter and early spring, but winter-flowering viola (pansies) can be relied upon to put up a good show. Sow them now, preferably in a cold frame, for planting out in the fall. Flowers will be produced in mild spells throughout the winter, with a bigger flush in early spring.

LEFT: **The cheerful yellow glow of marigolds will add life and color to your display of summer bedding plants.**

RIGHT: **Once the display of spring flowers is past its best, containers can be planted up with subjects to provide summer interest.**

Plant up containers

Colorful tubs, window boxes, and hanging baskets are immensely popular, and make very striking, long-lasting displays. Now that the risk of frosts is virtually over it should be safe to plant them and set them outside.

1 Garden centers usually have a good selection of suitable plants at this time of year. Select a variety of upright and trailing subjects, in a range of complementary colors; don't forget to include foliage plants as well as flowering ones.

2 Make sure that your containers have sufficient drainage holes, and enlarge them if necessary. Cover the drainage holes with a layer of coarse material such as large stones or crocks from broken clay pots to ensure that excess water can freely drain away (right).

3 Two-thirds fill the container with potting compost, and mix in some slow-release fertilizer and water-retaining granules (left). These absorb moisture and "hold" it in the mix, reducing the frequency of watering.

4 Arrange the plants, still in their pots, on the surface of the compost until the design is to your liking. Aim to balance tall, upright plants with trailing ones, and to achieve a harmonious combination of colors and foliage textures.

5 Use a trowel to plant up the container, filling in with more soil mix as necessary. Firm the plants well (above) and water them well. If possible, leave the planted containers in a sheltered, partially shaded place for a day or two before moving them to their final positions.

WATER GARDEN
PONDS

There is a water feature to suit every garden, no matter how small, and it is well worth taking the trouble to build one. Apart from the enjoyment you will gain from the sparkling water, the fish, and the colorful pond plants, all sorts of beneficial wildlife will be attracted to your garden pool as well.

Add moving water to ponds

A garden pool is always attractive, even when the reflective surface of the water is completely still—but it is even more enjoyable when the water moves. It sparkles and throws off light, making a pleasant splashing sound and helping to keep oxygen levels high for healthy fish and plants. Movement can be provided by fountains or waterfalls, and large pools can incorporate both. A submersible pump is the easiest way to power them. Fountain kits with a variety of heads for different effects are extremely easy to install once a power supply is made available (use a professional electrician for this). Waterfalls require a little more work. Natural-looking cascades can be tricky to build; avoid preformed fiberglass waterfall sections, and construct a water course lined with butyl, concealed by flat slabs of natural stone to provide the drops.

BELOW: **The splash of moving water, whether from a waterfall or a fountain, helps to bring a garden pool to life.**

Wildlife and the pond

A surprising variety of wildlife will find its way to your garden once a pool is established, and much of it will be helpful in your fight against garden pests. Frogs, toads, and newts eat large numbers of insects, and their feeding area extends much farther than the immediate environs of the pond. Birds, which are also valuable pest controllers, will visit the pond in order to drink and bathe, and slug-munching predators will quench their thirst here, too. The spectacular dragonflies that can be seen darting over the surface are not only colorful and attractive but fearsome insect predators.

How to make a garden pond

Late spring is the perfect time of year to construct and stock a garden pool. It's an easier process than many people think, and a pond enhances any style of garden. Always site a pool in an open, sunny position, away from overhanging trees.

1 Select the type of pond base you require. Molded fiberglass ponds are popular (above), but there is a restricted choice of shapes and sizes. A flexible liner can be used for any shape of pool and is easy to transport home. Butyl rubber has the longest life, but laminated PVC is cheaper.

2 Mark out the shape of the pool with rope or a trickle of sand (above); simple, flowing shapes are best. Excavate the soil to the correct depth, sloping the sides slightly and creating a shelf for marginal plants some 10in/25cm wide and 8in/20cm below water level. Check that the top of the pond is absolutely level.

3 You should then remove sharp stones or any other objects that may puncture the liner and cover the base and shelves of the excavation with a smooth layer of sand (above). Stretch the liner across the hole; however, it is important not to try to drape the liner into it. You should then weight down the liner edges with bricks.

ABOVE: Ponds will look after themselves as long as you get the right balance between plants, the wildlife and water. Make a pool as large as you can, with a minimum depth of 2ft/60cm: very small ponds are the most difficult to keep in good condition.

4 Lay a hose in the center of the liner and turn the water on (above). The weight of water will gradually stretch the liner and pull it into the hole, molding it to fit the excavation perfectly. Once the pond is full, trim away surplus liner to leave a 6in/15cm margin all around, which can be concealed with a stone edging to the pool.

WATER GARDEN
PLANTS AND FISH

Fish are not essential in a garden pond, but they add a great deal of interest to it and will prevent mosquitoes becoming a problem. Aquatic plants such as nymphaea (water lilies) are often the crowning glories of a pool; this is the perfect time to plant them, or to divide existing plants.

Introduce fish to garden pools

Any area of still water is likely to be visited by mosquitoes for the purpose of laying eggs, and once the eggs hatch the resulting swarms of insects can make life in the garden irritating and very unpleasant.

Adding fish to the pond provides the perfect answer; they will eat the larvae as soon as they hatch and prevent them reaching adulthood. They are also very attractive, and add life and movement to the water.

Goldfish are the most common type of fish for ponds, as they are cheap and easy to buy, and usually problem-free.

Golden Orfe are also popular with their long, slender shapes and attractive, light gold color. Shubunkins are a type of goldfish which have shades of silver, blue, red, brown, and black, while Fantails have attractive double tails.

The recommended stocking rate for fish to keep their environment healthy is three to five fish per square yard/ meter of surface area of water.

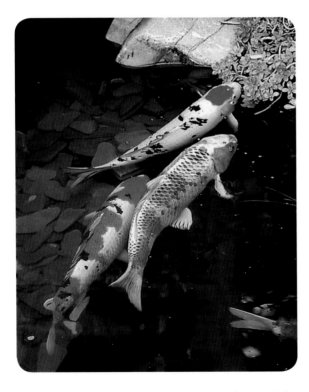

ABOVE: **When stocking fish ponds, it is important to bear in mind the recommended stocking rate of three to five fish per square yard/meter.**

Divide deep-water aquatics

Aquatic plants such as nymphaea (water lilies) and *Aponogeton distachyos* (water hawthorn) eventually grow too large for their planting baskets, and this has a detrimental effect on their growth and flowering. They can be divided at this time of year, giving you extra plants while improving the existing ones. Lift the basket out of the water (it may take two people) and remove the plant; very overgrown plants may need to have the basket cut away. Divide the plant into smaller sections, each with a healthy growing point. You may need a sharp spade or knife to cut the rootstock. Replant the sections in new baskets of good loam topped with grit. Return them to the pool.

Plant aquatics in ponds

The right mix of plants is vital to keep water gardens healthy. Oxygenating plants such as *Elodea canadensis* (Canadian pondweed) are essential to keep the water clear, but aquatics with floating leaves, such as water lilies and water hawthorn, also have an important part to play.

1 Line a perforated plastic planting basket with a piece of ordinary sacking (above) and then fill it with good quality, fertile, loamy soil.

2 Plant the aquatic in the soil, firm in, and water thoroughly. Cover the exposed surface soil with gravel or pebbles to prevent it from being washed away (above).

3 Gently lower the basket into the pool until it is resting on the bottom or shelf (above). Using planting baskets is better than planting direct into a layer of soil at the base of the pool as you can remove and trim plants more easily.

4 Oxygenating plants are often sold as bunches of unrooted stems, and attaching a small piece of lead weight helps prevent them from floating to the surface. They root quickly though if the bases of the bunches are firmed into wet soil in the planting baskets (below).

ABOVE: **Feed pond fish with specially formulated food through spring and summer, but remove any food that remains uneaten after 10 minutes.**

5 Varieties of nymphaea (water lily) vary in the optimum depth of water they require. Those that require shallow conditions can be planted in deeper areas by setting the planting basket on bricks or blocks to raise its height.

KITCHEN GARDEN
SOWING AND PLANTING

Crops in the kitchen garden are growing apace. If the weather is dry, some are likely to need watering to keep them growing strongly, but it's important to know when to water. It should now be safe to sow pole beans in the open: by the time the seedlings appear, frosts should be a thing of the past.

Sow pole and bush beans outdoors

The soil should now be warm enough for bean seeds to germinate quickly, and by the end of late spring, the seedlings should be safe from frosts. Dwarf bush beans are sown in single rows, spaced some 3in/7.5cm apart. Climbing bush beans and pole beans need supports, and they are generally put in place before sowing; a double row of bamboo canes, crossing at the top, works well. High yields have also been obtained from rows of canes

ABOVE: **Flowers on pole bean plants sometimes fall without setting pods. This is generally due to dry soil conditions; watering will cure the problem.**

Water vegetables as required

A dry spell at this time of year can result in a check to the growth of young plants, and watering may be necessary. Leafy vegetables such as cabbage and spinach respond well, giving an increased yield at harvest time if they have received a steady water supply throughout the growing season. All transplanted vegetables should be watered after planting until they are well established. Other vegetables, however, should not be watered too soon because watering stimulates leafy growth that may be at the expense of flowering and crop production. Beans and peas should not normally be watered until they have started to flower (unless the plants are actually wilting), but once flowering begins, regular watering will help the flowers to set and promote the formation of a good supply of tender beans.

spaced 2ft/60cm apart, with canes 12in/30cm apart in the row, sowing two seeds at the base of each cane.

There are many varieties of bush and pole beans available. With dwarf bush beans, look for varieties that hold their pods well clear of the ground because this avoids beans being eaten by slugs or spoiled by soil splashes. Purple- or gold-podded varieties are easy to pick because the beans are more visible. Stringless varieties of pole bean are popular because the pods are more tender, and stay in good condition longer.

Plant vegetables in containers

Not everyone has room for a vegetable plot, but almost every garden has sufficient space for a few vegetables in pots and growing bags on the patio. If the right varieties are chosen, the harvest can be surprisingly good. When using pots and tubs, ensure they have sufficient drainage holes and place a layer of crocks or other coarse drainage material at the base before filling with compost.

1 Prepare tubs and large pots in the normal way. Ensure that there are sufficient drainage holes and place a layer of crocks or other coarse drainage material over the base before adding soil mix. The mix can be soilless or loam-based, as you prefer.

2 Tomatoes, eggplants (above) and sweet peppers are among the most commonly grown vegetables in tubs, and young plants that have been hardened off can be planted out now. Add water-retaining granules to the soil mix to cut down the amount of watering required.

3 Growing bags can also be used for vegetables other than tomatoes (above). A bush-type zucchini plant (one per bag as they grow quite large) will give a good crop, and try pole beans in growing bags placed at the base of fences or walls for the plants to climb up. Both crops need frequent watering.

4 Other vegetables that can be tried in tubs or growing bags include potatoes, beets, kohlrabi, carrots, bush beans (above), lettuce, and radish. Choose fast-maturing, compact-growing varieties—there are several which have been bred specifically for containers on patios or balconies.

LEFT: **Zucchini make excellent subjects for a growing bag, but they will need frequent and careful watering.**

KITCHEN GARDEN
PESTS AND DISEASES

Birds are normally welcome garden visitors, helping to keep a wide variety of insect pests under control. Unfortunately, they also have less social habits and can be a real nuisance in the kitchen garden when they start eating the crops. Particularly susceptible crops should be protected now.

Protect crops from birds

Much as we like to see wild birds visiting the garden, they become distinctly unpopular when they start wreaking havoc among developing food crops. The soft fruit season will soon be at its peak, and many birds—particularly blue jays—are just as fond of the juicy fruits as we are, demolishing raspberries and strawberries with amazing speed. Peas are also at risk: colorful, noisy jays are often the main culprits here.

Where possible, protect susceptible crops with netting, ideally in the form of a fruit cage to allow easy access. Strawberries can be protected with low polyethylene or netting tunnels. Where netting and fruit cages are not practical, bird scarers can be tried, as shown later on page 125.

ABOVE: **The soft fruit season is probably the favorite for birds. You will need to protect your garden to prevent them feasting on your crops.**

Protect fruit from maggots

Most people will have had the experience of biting into an apparently perfect apple only to find extensive maggot damage. The usual culprit is the larva of the codling moth, and the adults are on the wing any time now. Chemical control of the moth is difficult, but damage reduction can usually be achieved biologically with pheromone traps. They are hung in the trees and lure the male moths to the trap by the use of female pheromones; sticky paper inside the trap ensures that the males cannot escape and breed. Such traps were originally used by commercial growers to indicate the best times to use insecticide sprays, but in the garden they can be used as an effective control.

Protect strawberries

Strawberries are a favorite delicacy for many gardeners but without some timely precautions birds, slugs or disease are likely to devour them before we get the chance. Now is the time to take action to protect the crop, well before the fruits start to ripen.

1 Strawberries are vulnerable to damp conditions, soil splashes and attack by a range of soil-based pests. This is a good time to surround the plants with clean straw (above), tucking it well under the crowns to keep the developing fruit dry and clear of the soil.

2 Where straw is not easy to obtain, fiber or polyethylene mulching mats or sheets can be used instead (above). They prevent soil splashes and suppress weed growth, but are not so good at keeping slugs and other pests at bay.

3 Garden birds are extremely partial to strawberries and will be drawn like a magnet when the fruit starts to redden. The only reliable way to protect the plants is by netting (above), but as strawberries are so low-growing this is not too difficult or expensive.

4 There is no point in simply throwing netting over the plants because the fruit will still be accessible to birds. Strawberry cages are available, or you can make a framework of canes or plastic poles to support the netting over the plants. Arrange the netting so that it will be quick and easy to remove and replace at picking time.

5 Where birds cause a lot of damage it might be worth investing in a walk-in fruit cage in which all kinds of soft fruit, such as currants, strawberries, raspberries and blueberries, can be grown safely. Although initially expensive, such a cage is definitely worth it for large crops.

LEFT: Silver leaf is a common disease of plums. Badly affected branches should be pruned back until they no longer show a brown stain in the wood.

SPRING
TASKS & PLANT OVERVIEW

Early spring tasks

GENERAL
- Prepare the soil for sowing when the weather allows
- Remove weeds and apply a moisture-retaining mulch

ORNAMENTAL GARDEN
- Plant container-grown trees and shrubs, and plant and divide herbaceous perennials
- Support border plants as soon as the shoots start to lengthen
- Sow hardy annuals and *Lathyrus odoratus* (sweet peas) outdoors
- Prune roses and shrubs such as buddleja, hydrangeas, and *Cornus alba* (dogwood)
- Remove winter protection from plants
- Fertilize spring-flowering bulbs, perennials, and shrubs if not already done
- Mulch round alpine plants with fresh gravel
- Trim back winter-flowering calluna (heathers)

LAWNS
- Begin mowing regularly; continue to carry out repairs to turf

KITCHEN GARDEN
- Dig up the last of the overwintered crops and sow early crops in their place
- Plant early potatoes, rhubarb, and shallots
- Continue harvesting rhubarb and kale
- Stake fall or early spring-sown beans and peas
- Protect early blossom on fruit trees
- Plant soft-fruit bushes
- Check raspberry supports

Mid-spring tasks

GENERAL
- Control weeds, slugs, snails and other pests as they appear
- Check plants that appear to have been killed by frosts

ORNAMENTAL GARDEN
- Plant summer-flowering bulbs and dead-head spring bulbs. Buy bedding plants from garden centers
- Continue to sow hardy annuals
- Take cuttings of border plants
- Plant *galanthus* (snowdrops) "in the green" (while in leaf)
- Check for reverted shoots on variegated shrubs
- Check for rose diseases and treat as necessary
- Plant alpines and evergreens
- Prune spring-flowering shrubs such as forsythia after flowering

LAWNS
- Apply a "weed and feed" combined herbicide and fertilizer
- Mow and edge lawns as necessary
- Deal with worm casts and moss
- Make new lawns from seed

WATER GARDEN
- Begin excavation work for a new pond

KITCHEN GARDEN
- Continue sowing successional crops. Prepare the trench for pole beans
- Sow winter brassicas outdoors
- Hoe off weeds regularly
- Plant out leeks and onion sets
- Earth up potatoes and plant second early and maincrop varieties
- Spray fruit with fungicide if mildew has been a problem in previous years
- Avoid spraying fruit trees with insecticides while pollinating insects are active
- Prune plums

Late spring tasks

GENERAL
- Check for pests on plants and treat promptly
- Feed strong growing plants
- Treat perennial weeds with herbicide

ORNAMENTAL GARDEN
- Plant up hanging baskets, window boxes, and tubs
- Continue staking border plants
- Weed annual seedlings and thin them as necessary
- Remove spring bedding plants; plant out summer bedding
- Plant dahlias
- Dead-head narcissus (daffodils).
- Water recently planted trees and shrubs if the weather is dry
- Trim evergreen hedges as necessary

LAWNS
- Lower the height of the mower blades to give a closer cut. Tackle weeds with a spot weed killer

WATER GARDEN
- Construct and plant up new ponds.
- In existing ponds, divide deep-water aquatics and plant new varieties
- Watch for aphids on water lily leaves, and submerge affected leaves to allow fish to eat them

KITCHEN GARDEN
- Water as necessary, timing the watering carefully for maximum crops
- Continue to make successional sowings for continuity of supply
- Plant out hardened-off pole and bush beans once the risk of frost is over. Sow pole beans and bush beans outdoors
- Thin out seedlings in the rows. Thin carrots and stake peas
- Plant vegetables in pots and growing bags
- Check plums for silver leaf disease
- Reduce codling moth damage with pheromone traps
- Straw around strawberries and net the plants against birds

LEFT: A fresh dressing of gravel around alpine plants helps to show the developing flowers off to perfection.

Ornamental plants in season

Early spring

TREES AND SHRUBS

Acer pseudoplatanus 'Brilliantissimum' (sycamore), *A. rubrum* (red maple)

Calluna 'Spring Cream', *C.* 'Spring Torch' and others (heather)

Camellia japonica (common camellia)

Chaenomeles speciosa, C. japonica (japonica)

Chimonanthus praecox (winter sweet)

Clematis armandii

Cornus mas (cornelian cherry)

Corylopsis pauciflora

Erica carnea varieties (winter heath)

Forsythia intermedia, F. suspensa

Magnolia stellata (star magnolia)

Prunus cerasifera pissardii (cherry plum)

Salix caprea (willow)

PERENNIALS AND BEDDING PLANTS

Aubrieta

Bergenia cordifolia

Doronicum (leopard's bane)

Primula vulgaris and others (primrose)

Pulmonaria (lungwort)

BULBS

Anemone (wind flower)

Bulbocodium vernum

Chionodoxa (glory of the snow)

Crocus

Cyclamen coum

Eranthis (winter aconite)

Erythronium (dog's tooth violet)

Iris danfordiae, I. reticulata

Leucojum vernum (spring snowflake)

Muscari (grape hyacinth)

Narcissus (daffodil)

Pushkinia scilloides

Tulipa kaufmanniana, T. fosteriana, T. tarda and others (tulip)

Mid-spring

TREES AND SHRUBS

Acer pseudoplatanus 'Brilliantissimum' (sycamore), *A. rubrum* (red maple)

Amelanchier lamarckii (juneberry)

Berberis darwinii, B. stenophylla (barberry)

Ceanothus (Californian lilac)

Clematis alpina, C. armandii

Cytisus praecox (broom)

Daphne burkwoodii, D. cneorum

Forsythia

Kerria japonica

Magnolia soulangiana, M. stellata (star magnolia)

Malus (apple, crab apple)

Osmanthus burkwoodii, O. delavayii

Pieris

Prunus in variety (ornamental cherry)

Rhododendron

Ribes sanguineum (flowering currant)

Rosmarinus officinalis (rosemary)

Spiraea arguta (bridal wreath)

Ulex europaeus (furze)

Vinca major (greater periwinkle), *V. minor* (lesser periwinkle)

PERENNIALS AND BEDDING PLANTS

Aurinia saxatilis

Aubrieta

Bellis perennis (common daisy)

Bergenia

Erysimum cheirii (wallflower)

Doronicum (leopard's bane)

Epimedium (barrenwort)

Euphorbia characias, E. polychroma

Helleborus orientalis (lenten rose)

Iberis sempervirens (candytuft)

Myosotis (forget-me-not)

Primula (primrose)

BULBS

Anemone

Bulbocodium vernum

Chionodoxa (glory of the snow)

Convallaria majalis (lily-of-the-valley)

Erythronium revolutum (American trout lily)

RIGHT: **The stately chalices of** ***Magnolia soulangiana*** **blooms are often spoiled by late frosts in exposed positions.**

Fritillaria imperialis (crown imperials), *F. meleagris* (snake's head fritillary)

Leucojum vernum (spiking snowflake)

Muscari (grape hyacinth)

Narcissus (daffodil)

Tulipa (tulip)

Late spring

TREES AND SHRUBS

Aesculus hippocastanum (horse chestnut)

Berberis (barberry)

Buddleja globosa

Ceanothus (Californian lilac)

Cercis siliquastrum (Judas tree)

Choisya ternata (Mexican orange blossom)

Clematis montana and large-flowered hybrids

Crataegus (hawthorn)

Crinodendron hookerianum

Davidia involucrata (handkerchief tree)

Deutzia gracilis, D. rosea

Genista hispanica (Spanish gorse)

Kerria japonica

Kolkwitzia amabilis (beauty bush)

Laburnum

Magnolia soulangiana

Malus (apple, crab apple)

Paeonia (peony)

Pieris

Potentilla fruticosa (cinquefoil)

Prunus (ornamental cherry)

Rhododendron (including azaleas)

Robinia hispida, R. margaretta

Rosmarinus officinalis (rosemary)

Sambucus racemosa plumosa 'Aurea' (red-berried elder)

Sorbus aria (whitebeam), *S. aucuparia* (mountain ash)

Spiraea arguta (bridal wreath)

Syringa (lilac)

Viburnum opulus (guelder rose), *V. plicatum* (Japanese snowball bush)

Weigela

Wisteria

PERENNIALS AND BEDDING PLANTS

Ajuga reptans

Aurinia saxatilis (*Alyssum saxatile*) (gold dust)

Aquilegia (columbine)

Armeria (sea pink)

Aubrieta

Dicentra spectabilis (bleeding heart)

Euphorbia (spurge)

Geranium

Helianthemum (rock rose)

Iberis (candytuft)

Lithodora diffusa

Primula (primrose)

Saxifraga umbrosa

BULBS

Allium (onion)

Anemone (windflower)

Hyacinthoides non-scripta (English bluebell)

Convallaria majalis (lily-of-the-valley)

Fritillaria imperialis (crown imperial)

Hyacinthus (hyacinth)

Leucojum aestivum (summer snowflake)

Tulipa (tulip)

EARLY SUMMER

 The garden retains the freshness of spring while the floral bounty of summer starts to unfold. While there's still plenty to do, the hectic spring rush is calming down, and we can enjoy the garden at a more leisurely pace, especially as the daylight hours stretch out into the evening now.

While everyone longs for a good spell of settled, warm, sunny weather, we also need enough rain to keep the plants growing strongly but droughts do seem to be becoming more common every year. Early summer is often a time of mixed weather with heavy storms depositing gallons of water on the garden within a few minutes, but gardeners need to be prepared to get out the hose or watering can if the weather remains dry for more than a few days.

At least, though, it's safe to stop worrying about damaging night frosts, and all those tender plants can now go outside, but do take care to harden them off properly first. Conditions should be near perfect for plant growth, and fast-growing plants now need regular care to keep them tied into their supports.

The early spring-flowering shrubs such as forsythia have had their moment of glory, and once the flowers are over it's time to think about pruning the plants. Roses will soon be in full bloom, but all too often the display is spoiled by pests and diseases. The latter can be prevented by regular fungicide sprays, and plants must be checked regularly for pests and treated with the appropriate controls as soon as any are spotted.

The perfect foil for burgeoning flower borders is an emerald-green lawn. Keep the lawn watered, fed and regularly mown (not too short) for the best results. The vegetable garden should now be producing an increasing number of crops to harvest; this is the time of year when they really taste their best. Toward the end of the summer the strawberries will be ready for picking, with the promise of raspberries and the rest of the soft fruit crop soon to follow.

ORNAMENTAL GARDEN
GENERAL TASKS

Herbaceous flower borders reach their peak later this period and into midsummer, but there is work to be done now to make sure they look their best. Stake or tie in those plants that need it, and keep weeds in the borders under control. Climbing plants also need care and attention.

Take cuttings from pinks

Pinks are very popular garden plants. They make neat, low cushions of growth with attractive silver-gray leaves; the flowers are freely produced in a wide range of red, pink, and cream shades, and many varieties are strongly fragrant. The plants are ideal for the front of the border, pots and containers, and rock gardens.

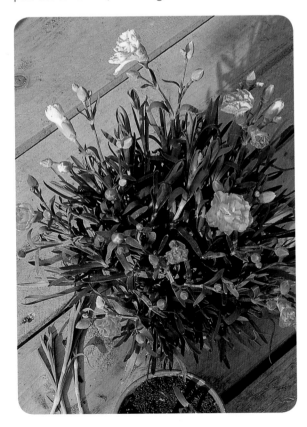

ABOVE: **Garden pinks (dianthus) can be propagated easily from cuttings known as "pipings," which are inserted into a sandy, free-draining soil mix.**

Pinks are also very easy to propagate. They are increased from cuttings that are known as "pipings." The stem has a swollen joint where each pair of leaves clasps it; if the stem is held just below one of these joints and the top part of the stem is tugged gently, it will pull out cleanly at the leaf joint to form a ready-made cutting. Make the pipings 3–4in/7.5–10cm long; they need no further trimming and can be inserted straight into pots of moist seed and cuttings mix, and firmed in well. The ideal place to root them is in a lightly shaded cold frame where they can remain over the winter.

Tie in border plants

This is a job that needs to be done frequently— if the shoots are allowed to get too long it is impossible to tie them back into the supports without giving the plant a misshapen appearance. Provide several canes if necessary for spreading plants, and tie individual stems to them. It is often necessary to use long pieces of twine in order to achieve a natural- looking shape: keep these as low on the stems as possible, where they will be less noticeable. Plant breeders are increasingly producing lower growing, stocky varieties of border plants, but even these will usually be improved by a little judicious support to keep them in shape.

Train and support climbers

Climbing plants add an extra dimension to a garden. They make use of vertical surfaces such as walls and fences, making them more attractive features; the surfaces also increase the overall amount of growing space, particularly valuable in small gardens. Proper support and training are essential.

3 Train the shoots of the plant as they grow, aiming to cover the support evenly. Tie the shoots in place with raffia, soft garden twine or plastic-coated metal ties, taking care not to tie them too tightly— ideally make a figure-of-eight loop with the tie to avoid damaging the stems (above).

1 A wooden trellis is a popular choice for supporting a climber on a wall; it should be treated with a plant-safe wood preservative and allowed to dry thoroughly. Attach wooden battens to the wall and then screw the trellis panel onto the battens (above), or attach it with hooks and eyes. This enables the trellis and climber to be removed carefully when wall maintenance is necessary.

2 An alternative support is horizontal, plastic-covered wires stretched taut between vine eyes screwed into the vertical surface. Space the vine eyes every 6ft/1.8m along the wall in rows 18in/45cm above each other and screw them in firmly. Loop the wire through the eyes, twisting it at each end to secure it. Tension the wire by turning the vine eye with pliers (above).

4 Several climbers are particularly attractive when allowed to scramble through the branches of trees and shrubs, but avoid very vigorous varieties which will smother their host. A classic combination is *Tropaeolum speciosum* (flame nasturtium) growing through a dark conifer.

Mulch borders

Clear all weed growth from borders and ensure the soil is thoroughly moist before applying a thick mulch of bark, cocoa shell or mushroom compost, etc. to prevent further weed growth and retain soil moisture through the summer.

ORNAMENTAL GARDEN
DIVIDING AND PLANTING

As some of the earlier-flowering garden plants reach the end of their season, it is time to give them a new lease of life by dividing them. And now that the risk of frosts is over, tender bedding plants can safely be set outside in their flowering positions to provide lush colors.

Divide and replant irises

Flag irises make a large, spreading clump once they have been established for several seasons, and the center of the clump can become bare and woody. Once they have finished flowering, plants can be lifted and divided, improving their performance for the following year. Dig up the clump of rhizomes carefully. Identify sections of rhizome around the edge of the clump that have strong young shoots and plenty of fibrous roots, and cut these out using a sharp knife. Discard the old, woody portions. Trim the leaves back to a fan shape about 9in/23cm long and then replant the sections of rhizome in groups of three or five, spacing them some 6in/15cm apart. The top half of the rhizome should remain above ground when planted.

ABOVE: **Once the blooms of flag irises have faded, established clumps of plants can be lifted and replanted to improve next year's performance.**

Lift and divide narcissus (daffodils)

Daffodil bulbs are usually left in the ground from year to year, but those that have been growing undisturbed for several years may start to deteriorate, sometimes becoming "blind" when they produce foliage but no flowers. When this happens it's often because they have become overcrowded, in which case you should lift and replant the bulbs.

Once the foliage has died down, lift the bulbs carefully with a garden fork and shake off the soil. Many will have formed offsets—smaller bulbs around the edge of the main bulb that eventually separate. When the offsets are large enough they will come away easily from the main bulb and can be removed. Replant all the bulbs at the correct spacing, having dug over the planting site first and added a little slow-release fertilizer to the soil.

Plant out tender bedding plants

Many favorite bedding plants are frost tender, and they can't be planted outside until all risk of frosts is over. They are often on sale in garden centers much too early. Tender bedding plants need to be hardened off (i.e. gradually acclimatized to outdoor conditions) before they are planted out in their flowering positions.

Keep them in a greenhouse, conservatory or other frost-free place at night, moving them outdoors during the day, until it is safe to plant them out.

1 Before planting, prepare the beds and borders where the plants are to grow by forking the soil over thoroughly, removing any weeds. Add an application of general fertilizer and work it into the top layer of soil.

2 Water the bedding plants well the evening before you intend to plant them. When planting, remove the plants from their pots or trays by giving the container a sharp knock on a firm surface to loosen the root ball; tease the plants apart carefully if necessary (right).

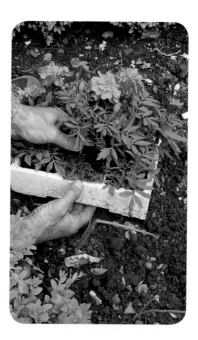

3 Plant with a trowel immediately they have been removed from the container (below)—do not leave the roots exposed to the air because they will dry out quickly and this will delay re-establishment. Firm the plants down into position thoroughly, using your knuckles.

4 Once the bed is planted, water the plants well using a fine rose on the end of the hose or watering can (below). Since the weather is often dry and warm at this time of year, frequent watering may be necessary, especially in the days immediately after planting.

ABOVE: **Nasturtiums and marigolds provide an attractive mixture of colors, especially highlighted when planted close together.**

ORNAMENTAL GARDEN
PRUNING AND TRIMMING

Several shrubs whose flowers are now finished will benefit from pruning. Other plants will also be bearing faded flowers, and dead-heading is an important job from now onward to keep the garden looking good. It's also time to give hedges a trim to keep them neat and tidy.

Prune early-flowering shrubs

There are several shrubs which flower in late spring and early summer whose season is now over. They include plants such as ceanothus, cytisus (broom), deutzia, kerria, philadelphus (mock orange), spiraea, syringa (lilac), viburnum and weigela.

These shrubs do not need annual pruning, but if they are becoming overgrown and untidy, now is a good time to tackle them.

Start as always by removing dead and diseased stems, then prune out remaining stems which are old, weak or badly placed. Use secateurs or a pruning saw to cut them off at ground level. Up to one-third of the stems can be removed to thin out the growth, and allow light and air into the center of the shrub.

RIGHT: **Spring-flowering shrubs such as lilac should have old and weak stems removed to allow light and air into the center of the plant.**

Dead-head plants as necessary

The aims of dead-heading are threefold—to prevent the garden from looking untidy, to conserve the strength of the plant by preventing it setting seed unnecessarily, and to encourage the production of further flowers. Plants grown for their fruit, berries or seedheads should obviously not be dead-headed.

Most plants should have the dead flowerheads snapped off or cut with secateurs just above a leaf joint; one exception is the rhododendron (including the azalea). This forms new buds immediately behind the old flowers, so the dead flowers must be removed very carefully by hand.

Trim hedges

Hedge clipping is not the most popular garden chore, but it gives a very satisfying result when it is done properly, and it is worth taking a little time and trouble to get it right. Most hedges need trimming twice a year, now and in late summer.

1 Clearing up will usually be quicker and easier if a tarpaulin or strong plastic sheet is laid beneath the hedge to catch the clippings (above). Where the hedge adjoins a flowerbed or border, a strip of paving slabs running directly alongside the base of the hedge is far easier to work from than the soil of the flowerbed.

2 For a formal hedge, stretch a piece of level twine tautly along the top of the hedge to ensure it is cut to a straight line (above). The top of the hedge can be left flat, but cutting it to a pointed shape (like a rooftop) is also attractive, and helps prevent damage from snow in areas that have severe winters.

3 Hand shears are satisfactory for small hedges, but powered hedge trimmers make the job quicker and easier (above). Electric trimmers are popular, but great care must be taken to ensure that the power cable is kept out of the way of the blades, and that a ground-fault interrupter (GFI)—or circuit breaker—is fitted.

4 Begin cutting the hedge from the base, working upward. The sides should slope slightly toward the top, making a wedge shape (above). When trimming tall hedges, use a sturdy pair of steps set parallel to the hedge to reach the top. Avoid leaning ladders or steps against the hedge because they will ruin its shape.

LEFT: **Suckers from rose rootstocks can be identified by the larger number of leaflets. Dig right down to the root to pull the sucker off.**

LAWNS AND WATER GARDENS
GENERAL TASKS

A well-kept lawn sets off the entire garden, so it is even more important to keep the grass up to scratch now that the rest of the garden is reaching its peak. The weather may be one thing that is working against you in your efforts to keep the grass lush and green; moles are another problem.

Water lawns as necessary

Grass is rarely killed by drought, but a parched, brown lawn ruins the look of the garden and often becomes overrun by weeds. With care, you can keep a beautiful green lawn without wasting water—an important consideration in these days of increasingly frequent water shortages.

Increase the turf's drought resistance by applying a bulky top-dressing in the fall and by never cutting the grass too closely. Raise the height of the mower blades in dry weather. In dry spells, examine the grass closely. If it remains crushed where you walk instead of springing back up ("footprinting"), and the color of the grass is dull, it is time to water. Use an efficient sprinkler to apply a minimum of ½in/12mm of water at a time and water late in the evening to avoid loss by evaporation.

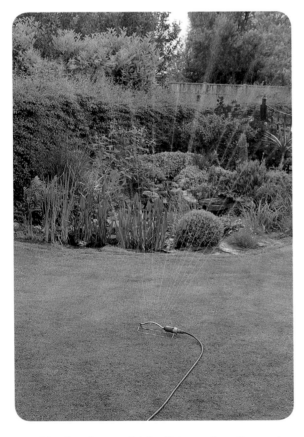

ABOVE: Watering a lawn too lightly will do more harm than good by encouraging roots to form in the upper, more drought-prone layers of the soil.

Deal with mole damage

Moles are one of the most frustrating garden pests. They can do terrible damage, particularly to lawns, and are almost impossible to control. Mole scarers are rarely effective, and mole traps kill just one mole whereupon others move into the vacant territory. The best thing to do is to grit your teeth until the mole has finished constructing his gallery of runs because tunneling then usually ceases. Sweep the molehills evenly over the lawn as soon as they appear—the soil makes a good top-dressing. Treat anthills in the same way. They are less disfiguring but if they are squashed flat by the mower, patches of grass will be killed and weeds will colonize the area.

Ant colonies can be treated with insecticide if really necessary.

Make a water feature

Water, especially moving water, is a great addition to any garden. A cobble or millstone water feature takes up little space, and is safe where there are young children. It also provides the sparkle and splash that makes water so entrancing. A competent electrician should provide the power supply to run the pump.

1 Excavate a hole to provide the water reservoir, making it at least 16in/40cm deep with a diameter some 12in/60cm wider than the millstone, incorporating a shallow lip all round the edge. Line the excavation with butyl rubber. A rigid fiberglass mold or plastic tank could be used instead.

2 Set a submersible pump at the base of the reservoir. Build two or three columns of bricks or concrete blocks in the center of the reservoir to take the weight of the millstone, and lay a rust-proof steel mesh over the top of them (right). The edges of the mesh are supported by the lip at the top of the reservoir.

3 Run a flexible pipe from the pump up the center of the millstone, with a rigid pipe to deliver the water at the top. This pipe should be set below the surface of the stone to obtain a bubbling spout rather than a jet of water. Arrange cobblestones on the mesh around the edge of the stone (below).

4 Fill the reservoir with water and switch on the pump, adjusting the flow to achieve the right effect. Water will bubble out of the center of the millstone and flow over the pebbles back into the reservoir, but it will need frequent topping up to make up for evaporation. Switching the pump off and allowing the stone to dry out regularly will help prevent the formation of algae on the stone.

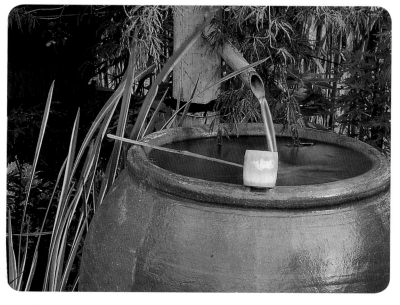

ABOVE: **Water plays an important role in Japanese gardens. This bamboo water feature adds an effective Far Eastern note.**

KITCHEN GARDEN
GENERAL TASKS

A range of pests and diseases can ruin the appearance of home-grown vegetables and fruit, but if you act promptly it is possible to protect plants against some of them. If you do not want to use chemical pesticides there are usually more environmentally friendly alternatives available.

Protect fruit against pests and diseases

Codling moth is probably the most troublesome apple pest prevalent at this time of year. The small adult moths fly at night and lay eggs on developing fruit and nearby leaves. When the larvae hatch, they make their way into the fruit and eat their way through it. Pheromone traps (see page 48) give some degree of control, but if you prefer a chemical remedy, an insecticide such as permethrin can be used in the middle of this month and again at the beginning of midsummer.

Also look out for gooseberry mildew that starts as a furry white coating on the shoot tips and young fruits, and soon develops into a dense brown felt on the fruits. A range of fungicides can be used to protect plants against the disease.

BELOW: **The dense brown felt that forms on mildewed gooseberry fruits can be rubbed off before cooking, but it is a time-consuming job.**

Caterpillars and brassica crops

Most gardeners like to see butterflies in the garden but few of them would welcome the cabbage white. It lays eggs on the leaves of any type of brassica, and they hatch out into ravenous caterpillars that can strip a plant bare in a few days. Hand picking and destroying the caterpillars is possible, but not very practical. A better bet is a biological control that is generally very successful. It combines spores and toxins from a natural bacteria, *Bacillus thuringiensis*. Once infected, the caterpillars die within a few days, but they stop feeding and damaging the plants immediately they have ingested the spray.

Earth up potatoes

When the young shoots of potato plants first appear above ground, drawing soil over them gives protection against a late frost. As the plants grow, continuing to earth up prevents bitter green patches forming on the tubers.

1 In cold regions a late frost can still occur in early summer. If potato shoots are just appearing through the soil and frost is forecast, draw soil up to cover the shoots completely. Alternatively, cover the shoots with sheets of newspaper or row covers held in place with soil or stones, but remove this the following day.

2 As the top-growth develops, continue to draw soil up the sides of the stems at regular intervals to form a ridge (right). This prevents tubers near the soil surface from being exposed to light that will turn them green; green tubers are inedible as they contain poisonous solanine, which causes severe stomach upsets.

3 As an alternative to the process of earthing-up potatoes can be grown under black poly mulch. Seed potatoes are planted in cultivated soil and black plastic sheeting is laid over the surface; as the shoots develop, slits are cut in the sheeting in the appropriate positions to allow the top-growth through.

4 The earliest potatoes are usually ready to harvest when the plants begin to flower. Scrape away a little soil to expose the tubers—they are ready to lift when they are the size of an egg (left). Yields are only small at this stage, but these early crops are particularly delicious.

Harvesting peas

Early sowings of peas should now be ready for picking. They are best harvested as soon as the peas reach a usable size—don't leave them to become too big or they get tough and starchy. Wait until the shapes of the peas are just visible through the pod. For the sweetest flavored peas, harvest the pods at an early stage, when the young peas inside them are just visible through the pod.

KITCHEN GARDEN
SOWING AND PLANTING

The sowing season for vegetables is not yet over. In fact there are several types that can be sown now to extend the season and provide crops in late summer. It's also time to think even farther ahead and plant out some of the vegetables that will see you through the winter days.

Sow successional crops

Although the main sowing season is over, there are several vegetables that can be sown successfully over the next few weeks for picking in late summer or early fall. They include radishes, carrots, beets, corn salad, lettuces, kohlrabi, arugula, radicchio, turnips, rutabaga, and spinach. Care should be taken with the choice of varieties as the summer wears on because some are more suitable for late-season sowing than others, being resistant to bolting, or diseases such as mildew.

Lettuce often fails to germinate when sown in summer because it is subject to high temperature dormancy. This means lettuce should be sown with extra care in hot spells. Water the drills well immediately before sowing to reduce the soil temperature, and sow in the cool of evening for the best results.

BELOW: **Fast-maturing radish can be sown at intervals all through the summer to provide a succession of young, tender roots.**

Plant out winter crops

Winter crops such as Brussels sprouts, cabbages, kale, and leeks can be planted out now. All brassicas (members of the cabbage family) need to be planted very firmly because loose planting leads to loosely formed heads without a dense heart, and "blown" sprouts. In all but very heavy soils, firm newly planted brassicas very thoroughly with the sole of your boot; firm again after watering. If you gently tug a leaf of the plant, the leaf should tear before the plant's roots move in the soil.

Plant peppers outdoors

Once the risk of frost is over, tender crops such as peppers (capsicums) and tomatoes can be planted safely out of doors. Make sure the young plants are thoroughly hardened off before setting them in their final positions.

1 Sturdy young plants that are filling an 3½in/8cm pot with roots are the best size for planting out. Select vigorous, healthy plants with deep green leaves; white root tips should be just visible through the drainage holes at the base of the pot.

2 Remove the plant from its pot by placing two fingers either side of the plant's stem, inverting the pot and knocking the rim against a hard surface, e.g., the edge of a table. The whole root ball should slide out of the pot easily (right).

3 Dig a hole with a trowel in well-prepared soil in the vegetable garden and set the plant in it (right), covering the top of the root ball with soil and firming in well with your knuckles and fingers. Water well immediately after planting.

4 If the weather should turn cool or windy after planting, young plants can be protected by covering them with a cloche. As the plants grow taller, two cloches can be turned on end to continue to provide some shelter.

5 Peppers and other tender vegetable crops also grow well when planted in growing bags on a patio (below), often a more sheltered position. Set two plants per bag for the best results. Cut a cross in the plastic and tuck the flaps under to make the planting hole. Plants in growing bags need regular watering and liquid feeding, particularly in dry or windy weather.

LEFT: **Green peppers are simply fruits picked when immature. If allowed, they will ripen to red, orange or yellow, according to variety.**

MIDSUMMER

Flowers are at their peak in most gardens now, and dead-heading, watering, staking, and harvesting will keep gardeners busy. Make the most of the good weather to enjoy the garden, and on warm nights make sure you stroll around after dusk to appreciate the night-scented flowers.

Lawn grasses are among the first plants to show distress in dry spells. Continue mowing the grass frequently to keep it looking good, but raise the height of the mower blades a little to give the lawn more drought resistance. As long as the clippings are very short, they can be left on the lawn in dry spells to help conserve moisture.

Rock garden plants and some early-flowering perennials will look better for being tidied up now, so once flowering has finished, cut them back hard. Continue to prune deciduous flowering shrubs after flowering, too, to keep them to the required size. Many shrubs can also be propagated from semi-ripe cuttings this month and next.

In the kitchen garden there should be plenty to harvest, but successional sowings continue to extend the season. Keep fruiting plants such as beans, marrows, and peas well watered while flowering to ensure a good crop.

Watering throughout the garden is likely to take up a considerable amount of time in midsummer, but take care to carry this task out thoroughly. Outdoor plants in containers, particularly, can start suffering from water shortage within hours on hot, cloudless summer days so ensure they are not allowed to dry out.

ABOVE: **Lupins are particularly prone to damage by heavy rain if they are not adequately staked. This variety is "Gallery Pink."**
OPPOSITE: **Lavender brings a splash of color to the garden, and contributes to the marvelous aromas at this time of year.**

Fungus diseases can be a particular problem in warmer weather, and a routine of preventive fungicide sprays is a good idea for susceptible plants. Pests should be treated as soon as they are seen.

MIDSUMMER
GENERAL TASKS

Watering is often vital during dry spells, but when incorrectly carried out it can do more harm than good. Most gardeners like to spend as much time as possible in their gardens now, and an outdoor lighting system enables gardens to be appreciated for that much longer each day.

Water garden plants with care

When watering any plants, it is important to make sure that the soil or compost is moistened right down to the main root area. If just a small amount of water is given it often penetrates only a shallow, top layer of soil; this encourages roots to form in this upper area, making the plant more prone to drought in the future. Water thoroughly or not at all!

BELOW: **A seep hose is an efficient and virtually labor-free way of applying water to the soil; hardly any water is lost by evaporation.**

Water can be applied in a number of different ways—with a watering can, through a hose pipe, by sprinkler or by seep hose. A seep hose is often one of the most efficient ways of watering because very little water is lost by evaporation. It is simply a length of tubing that is blocked at one end with holes at regular intervals along its length. It is laid on the soil alongside the plants and attached to a hose; water seeps out of the holes onto the soil. If there is a ban on garden sprinklers, remember that the ban includes seep hoses, too!

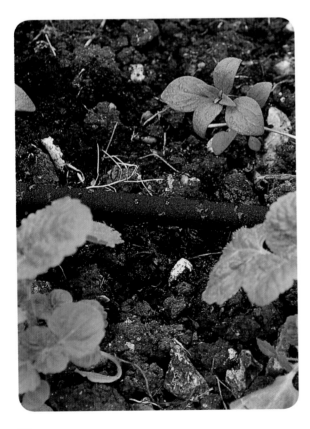

Stake border plants firmly

At this time of year heavy storms are not uncommon, and rain and hail can flatten plants in minutes. Even if the flowering stems are not broken, insufficiently supported plants are unlikely to recover their shape fully after such a downpour. As long as border plants have been firmly staked and regularly tied in to their supports, they are more likely to survive without serious damage.

Wet weather can cause buds to rot instead of opening fully; this is often seen on roses (particularly the full-flowered, old-fashioned varieties) and is known as "balling." Unfortunately there is little you can do to prevent it; cut off affected buds to encourage a second flush to form.

Prepare for holidays

The summer holiday season comes at just the wrong time for the garden, when everything is growing lushly and needs regular attention to keep it looking good. However, it is worth spending a little time in preparation before you leave to prevent you from being confronted by a depressing jungle on your return.

1 Gather all planted containers, including hanging baskets, together in one spot (right). Place them in a sheltered, partially shaded position. Add water-retaining granules to the soil mix if this has not already been done. Give them a thorough soaking before you go, but if you're away for more than a long weekend, ask a neighbor to water them every couple of days.

2 Mow the lawn just before you go, but do not be tempted to cut it more closely than normal because this will damage the turf and make it more prone to drought. If it is overlong on your return, reduce the height gradually over several cuts (below).

3 Weed flowerbeds and the vegetable plot thoroughly, hoeing to remove all seedling weeds. Applying a mulch to the soil will help prevent new weed growth and also keep the soil moist.

4 In the vegetable garden, pick all fruiting crops such as zucchini, peas, and pole and bush beans. Any left to mature on the plants will reduce future production, so arrange for a friend or neighbor to continue the harvest in your absence. Normally they are only too happy to oblige in return for the opportunity of a supply of fresh, home-grown produce!

Use garden lighting to advantage

The garden can be a dramatic place at night with the imaginative use of lights. Spotlights can highlight particular plants or ornaments of interest or form interesting shadows or silhouettes, while underwater lights can make a garden pond a magical feature. Lighting on the patio enables meals to be enjoyed out of doors after dark, and well-placed lighting can be an important safety feature on potential hazards such as paths and steps. Garden lighting kits are generally easy to install (see page 70), but if you have any doubts, employ a qualified electrician to do the job.

ORNAMENTAL GARDEN
GENERAL TASKS

Dahlias, one of the mainstays of late summer and fall, need attention now to produce prize-winning blooms. Another eye-catcher is the Madonna lily—look out for bulbs, which will be on sale soon. And why not extend the amount of enjoyment you get from the garden by installing lighting?

Install garden lighting

Low-voltage outdoor lighting systems are safe to use and easy to install. Complete kits are available containing everything you will need, including instructions, lamps, cables, and a transformer.

First, draw out a sketch of your lighting plan to estimate the amount of cable you will need, and to ensure you have enough. Find a suitable position for the transformer (see the instructions for precise details).

Lay the lamps in their appropriate positions, then run the cable between them, leaving a long loop at each lamp. Attach the cable to the lamps as instructed, then assemble the rest of the lighting fitting and push the lamps firmly into the ground. When all the lamps are attached, test the system to ensure it is working properly. If everything is in order, the cable running between the lamps can be buried under the soil, ensuring it is not likely to be disturbed by future digging.

ABOVE: **Low voltage garden lighting kits contain all you need to transform your garden into a magical place during the hours of darkness.**

Stake and disbud dahlias

Dahlias are important plants for providing color and form in the late summer and fall garden. If large, eye-catching flowers are required, they can be obtained by disbudding the stems. Leave just the terminal bud on each stem, and remove all the buds from the leaf axils below it by snapping them off or rubbing them out. This will need to be repeated several times. Each flowering stem will need to be provided with a sturdy stake, and must be tied in regularly. Earwigs can be a problem, chewing at the petals and spoiling the flower shape. They can be caught in traps consisting of a small pot filled with straw, inverted on the top of the stake. Inspect the traps each morning, and shake out and destroy any earwigs sheltering there.

Take semi-ripe cuttings

Now is a good time to take semi-ripe cuttings from many shrubs. They are less delicate than softwood cuttings, and need no special treatment. Most will be well rooted by the fall, but can be left in their trays in a sheltered place until the following spring.

1 Choose the current season's shoots which are still pliable, and just beginning to harden and become woody at the base. Cut the shoots with secateurs or, if small enough, tear them off the stem with a small sliver of bark attached.

2 Remove the lower leaves and, if necessary, trim the stem (right). The size of cutting varies from shrub to shrub, but is usually around 4in/10cm long.

3 Dip the base of the cutting in hormone rooting powder, tapping it once or twice to leave just a thin film on the stem.

4 Insert cuttings into prepared pots or trays of soil mix topped with a layer of sharp sand (left). Place the pots or trays in a cold frame if possible, or a well-ventilated greenhouse or a sheltered position outdoors. Keep them lightly shaded for the first few days or so.

Plant fall-flowering bulbs

Bulbs such as amaryllis and colchicum, which flower in the fall, can be planted now. Most fall-flowering bulbs prefer a sunny spot in a sheltered situation. The Madonna lily (*Lilium candidum*) should also be planted soon: this is actually summer flowering, but needs to be planted as early as possible for flowers next year. It is a particularly striking lily with large, pure white, heavily scented, trumpet-shaped blooms. Look out for the bulbs appearing in garden centers from now on. Unlike most other lilies the Madonna lily requires very shallow planting, with just 2in/5cm of soil above the tip of the bulb.

ORNAMENTAL GARDEN
PRUNING AND DEAD-HEADING

Plants are working hard to produce magnificent displays of flowers at the moment, and can easily wear themselves out after a short time. With the correct care, however, it is possible to extend the season so that you can continue to enjoy a garden full of color for as long as possible.

Care for containers

Tubs, window boxes, and hanging baskets have become an indispensable feature of most gardens in summer, spilling over with plants to provide color throughout the season. Because the plants are crowded in small volumes of soil mix, however, they soon begin to suffer from the effects of competition.

Containers need regular watering, feeding, and dead-heading in order to keep the plants flowering for the longest possible period. The amount of water they need depends on the type of mix in which they are growing and whether they are in a sheltered or exposed position, but it is often necessary to water small containers two or three times a day in hot, sunny weather. Add a dilute liquid feed to the water at every watering, or if you prefer you can incorporate some season-long, slow-release fertilizer granules into the soil. Dead-heading (where practical) will help to encourage further flushes of bloom.

BELOW: **A number of border plants that flower in late spring and early summer will produce a second flush of blooms if cut back after flowering.**

Cut back rock garden plants after flowering

Many of the rockery plants that were proving such a colorful spectacle a few weeks ago are looking rather bedraggled now that nearly all the flowers are over. Trim back species such as aubrieta, aurinia (alyssum), iberis and cerastium with secateurs or a pair of well-sharpened shears, cutting the shoots to around half their length. This encourages fresh new growth and keeps the plants neat and compact. It can sometimes result in a further flush of flowers to brighten up the rock garden later in the season, but should certainly improve the flowering of the plants next spring.

Prune wisteria

The glorious scented flowers of wisteria are over, but careful pruning now will help to ensure a spectacular display next year. Wisteria can be a difficult climber to grow well, sometimes seeming reluctant to flower profusely, but the correct pruning will greatly improve its performance. Remember that further pruning will be necessary in winter.

1 Wisteria flowers early, when the leaves are only just starting to open. By midsummer, however, the attractive pinnate foliage has made vigorous growth, and the leafy shoots may be getting out of hand (above).

2 Over the next few weeks, cut back nearly all the long shoots to about 6–10in/15–25cm from the main stem (above). Any stems needed to fill in the main framework can be pruned more lightly or left unpruned.

3 Climbing plants flower better when the flow of sap is slowed down by training the stems horizontally instead of letting them grow straight up. Pull the stems gently into a near horizontal position and tie them to the support (above).

4 Summer pruning is only half the story; the shoots you have just cut back will need pruning again in winter, reducing them to three buds from their base. This will help promote the production of flowering spurs.

5 Once summer pruning is completed, ensure the soil around the roots is moist and apply a mulch around the base of the plant (right). Wisteria prefers moderately rich, moisture-retentive, loamy soil. In dry soils, the flower buds may drop from the plant before they open fully.

LEFT: **A second flush of flowers from plants such as perennial geraniums will be especially welcome in a few weeks.**

KITCHEN GARDEN
GENERAL TASKS

There are not too many plant diseases that have a really devastating effect on crops, but potato blight is one of them. Take action as soon as you see the first signs of this disease. Also, tidy up strawberry beds now that the crop is over, and propagate the plants by rooting runners.

Potato blight

This disease is common in wet summers, and is remarkable for the speed with which it develops. The first signs are brown blotches on the foliage, sometimes with a white mold on the underside. Symptoms spread rapidly, and within a few days the entire top-growth of the plants may have yellowed and collapsed.

BELOW: **Keep a sharp look-out for the first signs of potato blight on the foliage. If action is taken straight away, the crop can usually be saved.**

Blight also affects the tubers, causing a dark brown rot. Spores infect the tubers when rain washes them off the top-growth into the soil. If the tubers are of a usable size, as soon as blight is identified on the foliage the top-growth should immediately be cut down and burned, removing all trace of it from the soil surface. Tubers may then escape infection.

In damp summers, especially if blight has occurred the previous year, it is worth giving potatoes a protective fungicide spray from midsummer onward.

Strawberry beds

When strawberry plants have finished cropping it is time to give the bed some radical treatment. At one time it was common practice to set light to the straw as it lay around the plants; the ensuing blaze burned up the leaves and frazzled any lurking pests and disease spores.

Risk of the flames getting out of hand is too great for this to be a popular method any longer, however. Instead, the leaves are cut from the plants, using a pair of shears or a nylon line trimmer: be careful not to damage the new growth in the center of the crowns. Rake up the cut foliage together with the straw, and remove it for burning in a safe place.

Root strawberry runners

As long as established strawberry plants are healthy and vigorous, it is easy to produce new plants to extend the bed or to replace old, worn-out plants. Strawberry plants naturally produce a profusion of runners which root quickly and easily.

1 Strawberry runners are freely produced. Long, creeping stolons extend from the plants, bearing two or three plantlets along their length. If not required for propagation, runners are normally removed regularly to prevent a mass of tangled growth (right).

2 Select four or five of the strongest, most vigorous runners for propagation and remove the rest. Spread the runners evenly around the plant.

3 The plantlet nearest the parent is always the strongest on the runner, and the ones beyond it should be nipped off and discarded. Plantlets can be rooted direct into the soil around the plant—simply weigh down the runner with a stone, or peg into the soil with a loop of wire to prevent it from being blown about (right).

4 Alternatively, the plantlets can be rooted into pots filled with either good quality garden soil or soil mix. Rooting the runners into pots makes the plants quicker to establish on transplanting as there is less root disturbance when the young plants are lifted. Either clay or plastic pots are suitable for this.

5 Half-bury the pots in the soil around the parent plant and peg the runners down into the mix (right). When pots are being used, it is important to make sure that the soil mix in them is not allowed to dry out.

Train outdoor tomatoes

For a good crop of outdoor tomatoes it is essential to choose varieties specifically recommended for outdoor culture. They may be grown as cordons like greenhouse tomatoes, or as bushes, depending on the variety selected. Cordon varieties need regular side-shooting and tying in to their support, but bush varieties generally do not. Some bush varieties are specially bred for growing in patio pots or even hanging baskets, where the stems cascade over the sides. They need no training, but frequent watering and regular feeding are necessary, as for all container-grown plants.

Between mid and late summer, the tops of cordon-grown plants should be pinched out to encourage the fruits to ripen.

Bush varieties form a sprawling mound and do not usually need staking or side-shooting.

KITCHEN GARDEN
PLANTING AND HARVESTING

Herbs are valuable in the garden for their appearance and fragrance, and indispensable in the kitchen. While nothing beats the flavor of fresh herbs, there are several easy ways in which they can be preserved. Midsummer, while they are at their peak, is the time to pick them for storing.

Harvesting herbs

The best time to pick herbs is in the morning of a dry day, waiting until the dew has dried off the foliage. Pick young stems, and try to avoid washing them unless it is absolutely essential.

The age-old method of preservation is drying; it is simple to do and gives good results. Tie the herbs in small, loose bunches—if they are too large, they will go moldy in the center. Hang them upside down in a warm, dry,

airy place. The atmosphere in the kitchen is usually too moist and an airing cupboard (with the door ajar), spare bedroom or garden shed may be more suitable. Once the stems and foliage are completely dry, the herbs can be crumbled and stored in tightly lidded jars.

For faster results, herbs can be laid on racks in a very cool oven overnight. They can also be dried in batches in a microwave, though it is often difficult to get the timing right with this method.

LEFT: **Select fresh, young shoots of herbs for preserving, picking them early in the morning, once the dew has dried off the leaves.**

Freezing herbs

Freezing tends to give fresher-tasting results than drying, and is particularly useful for herbs that do not dry well, such as basil.

Pick over the herbs and remove tough stems, then place them (single varieties or a mixture) in an electric blender and almost cover with water. Whizz them in the blender until the herbs are finely chopped, then pour the resulting mixture of herbs and water into ice cube trays and freeze. Add one or two of the ice cubes to soups, sauces or casseroles.

Plant out leeks

Leeks are an invaluable winter vegetable, withstanding almost any amount of cold weather. Seedlings from sowings made in trays or a seedbed in spring will now be ready for transplanting to their final positions.

1 Prepare the ground for leeks thoroughly, because they need to be planted deeply in order to develop the maximum length of tender white stems. The crop will benefit from some well-rotted compost or manure worked into the soil before planting.

2 Knock the underside of the seedtray smartly to loosen the roots, and tease the young plants apart carefully. Gather up a handful of seedlings with the bases of the plants in line, and trim the long, straggly roots and leaf tips with a pair of sharp scissors to make the plants easier to handle (below).

3 Make planting holes with a wooden dibber some 6in/15cm deep and the same distance apart. It's best to trim back the roots.

RIGHT: **Continue to keep the vegetable garden free of weeds as far as possible. Increasing numbers of crops are approaching maturity now.**

4 A leek seedling is simply dropped into each hole, leaving the holes open (below). Make sure the leek drops right to the base of the hole: that's why it's best to trim back the roots.

5 Once planting is complete, water the plants gently; this washes enough soil over the roots to anchor them in place. Each planting hole is filled with water and then left to drain (below).

6 If the weather is very dry shortly after planting, the seedlings may need to be watered again once or twice, but otherwise they usually need no further attention. They will be ready for harvesting in fall and winter.

LATE SUMMER

 The garden is at its best now, but despite the profusion of summer flowers and foliage, the first hints of fall soon make themselves felt. Dusk begins to come earlier, and in the mornings there is a hint of mistiness and heavy dew. It's time to start to prepare for the fall ahead.

In dry seasons, watering will be a priority in both the flower and kitchen gardens. Weeds may not be in such profusion as in early summer but must still be dealt with promptly if they are not to get out of hand.

Herbaceous and mixed borders can look splendid around this time, but weeding, mulching, staking, and tying in plants must continue. Staking is particularly important now because late summer storms can bring heavy rain and strong winds to wreck the display. Some of the border plants that were at their best earlier may now need to be trimmed in order to allow later-flowering subjects to be seen. Also take steps to control various pests and diseases before they have a chance to inflict too much damage—mildew on plants such as *Aster novi-belgii* (Michaelmas daisies) is very bad in some years, but can be kept at bay by regular fungicide spraying of susceptible subjects.

In the kitchen garden there is often a glut as all the crops come to fruition at once. Picking must continue regularly because if pods or fruits of crops such as beans, peas, zucchini, and marrows are allowed to mature, the plants will stop producing further crops. Surplus produce

ABOVE: **Among the best of the late-flowering border plants are the aromatic, flat, colorful heads of achillea.**

should be stored away for the winter and next spring, and now is the time for freezing, bottling, and jelly and pickle making.

This is also the time of year when many gardeners take a couple of weeks' holiday, leaving the garden to fend for itself. This need not mean facing disaster on the return home; a little work put in before the holiday will be more than repaid afterward.

ORNAMENTAL GARDEN
GENERAL TASKS

Walls and fences often mark the boundary of a garden, but they also have several other purposes. They provide protection from cold winds, keep out stray animals and trespassers, give privacy from neighbors and passers-by, and camouflage eyesores that detract from the pleasure of the garden.

Choosing the barrier

The type of screen that is most appropriate depends on the main purpose for which it is required. For protection against strong winds a solid barrier is not a good choice—the air rips over the top of the barrier and comes down the other side in gusts and eddies, often making the problem worse rather than curing it. A permeable barrier such as trelliswork with a light covering of plants, screen block walling or a post and rail fence is better in this situation, because it filters the wind and slows its speed.

For privacy, a solid barrier may be a better choice, though this depends on exactly how the garden is overlooked and by whom—a light, permeable screen may be sufficient to obscure the view from outside. The same applies to views that you wish to obscure from within the garden. Careful positioning of a screen is therefore very important. Moving the screen backward or forward between the object to be disguised and the viewpoint will make a substantial difference to the height or width the screen needs to be.

RIGHT: **A light wooden garden screen may be all that you need to provide some privacy in a garden that could be overlooked.**

Fences

Fences may be made of wood, plastic or wire, and prefabricated wooden panels are one of the most popular options. They are made from thin woven slats, or feather-edged boards arranged horizontally or vertically. The panels are fixed to timber or concrete uprights but being solid they are not the best option as windbreaks. Picket fences consist of vertical pieces of timber spaced along horizontal rails; they have an attractive appearance, being formal yet cottagey. Post and rail fences use two or three horizontal rails between uprights; they are relatively inexpensive but are useful only as boundary markers. Wire fences are not very attractive but are good at keeping out animals and trespassers. When clothed with climbing plants they also give a degree of wind protection and privacy.

Overwintering non-hardy perennials

Many popular garden plants are not frost hardy or not reliably so. They are often described as "slightly tender" or "dubiously hardy," and will die in a hard winter. Take some cuttings now and you will have young plants to act as an insurance policy against winter losses.

Plants that may be severely damaged by frost include pelargonium, many varieties of fuchsia, argyranthemum (marguerite), lantana, heliotropium (heliotrope) and *Helichrysum petiolare* among others. Cuttings usually root quickly at this time of year to provide plants for overwintering.

1 Select vigorous, healthy, preferably non-flowering shoots and either snap them off or cut them with secateurs. Trim off the lower leaves, and make a cut with a razor blade or sharp knife just below a leaf node (right).

2 Insert the prepared cuttings into sandy soil mix in a seed tray or around the edge of a pot (below). Water them well using a fine spray, and cover with a clear plastic propagator top. Keep them in a warm, lightly shaded position.

3 The propagator top can be removed or its ventilators opened once the cuttings show signs of rooting. They can remain in a frost-free greenhouse or conservatory, or a cool, bright room in the home, over the winter months.

Earwig traps

Check chrysanthemum and dahlia flowers for signs of earwig damage. These flowers are particularly prone to attack from earwigs, which eat holes in the petals, and distort the flowerheads by damaging the buds as they open. Night is the main feeding time, when most of the damage is done; during the day the earwigs seek a convenient place to hide. Earwig traps can be set up by inverting a flower pot loosely stuffed with straw on the end of a garden cane near the flowers. This provides an irresistibly attractive daytime roost for the pests that can be shaken out of the straw and disposed of.

ORNAMENTAL GARDEN
PLANTING AND POTTING

It's time to look ahead and replant exhausted summer-flowering containers for winter interest. Trees and shrubs can be planted now, too, but remember they need special care after planting in hot weather. And if you fancy some fresh mint for winter, this is the time to pot up a few roots.

Container-grown specimens

Both shrubs and border plants can continue to be planted right through the summer if they have been grown in containers, but it is important to remember to water them regularly.

Water the plants in their containers several hours or the day before planting. This ensures that the top-growth is fully charged with moisture and is able to cope with any disturbance with minimum wilting; it also aids the removal of the root ball from the pot without root damage. In hot, sunny weather, avoid planting during the middle of the day when the planting site is in full sun; it is better to wait until the relative cool of evening. Water the soil thoroughly immediately after planting: another watering a couple of hours later may be necessary to ensure the water penetrates right down to the roots.

RIGHT: **Containers come in many shapes and sizes; these stylish containers are made from old car lights.**

Pot up mint for winter

A few sprigs of fresh young mint are very welcome during the winter months, and potted roots are easy to encourage into growth while outdoor plants are completely dormant. The spreading roots of mint can be found just below the soil surface: using a trowel, lift a few long sections. They break easily, but even small portions of the roots will grow, and their removal will not harm the parent at all. Fill a seedtray with potting compost, firm it well, and press the lengths of mint root into the soil mix surface until they are covered. Cover with a further layer of soil and water until it is just moist. Keep the tray in a moderately warm place, either in the greenhouse or on a light windowsill in the home. Once the shoots start to appear, give them as bright a position as possible.

Plant a winter window box

By late summer, many containers of plants are starting to look a little jaded and past their best. Once this stage is reached it is a good time to replant some containers to give interest through the winter, when it will be especially welcome.

1 Remove and discard the worn-out bedding plants and soil. Clean out the inside of the window box, replace crocks over the drainage holes and refill the box loosely with fresh soil mix (right).

2 Select plants to give color, form, and flowers over the fall and winter. Suitable choices include winter-flowering heathers and viola (pansies), skimmia, dwarf conifers, variegated hedera (ivy), and small bulbs such as galanthus (snowdrops) and early-flowering crocus.

3 Set your chosen plants, still in their pots, in the window box until you have arranged them to your satisfaction. It is usually best to have taller, upright plants to give height toward the center of the box, and some trailers at the sides to soften the outline (below).

4 Remove the plants from their pots and set them in the window box using a trowel, adding further mix as necessary. Firm in lightly but thoroughly, using your knuckles. Bulbs such as snowdrops can be planted last, pushing them to the correct depth with a dibber (below).

5 Water the completed window box and put it in a sheltered place to establish for a few weeks (above): it can then be moved to its permanent position. Choose a place not exposed to extreme cold or winds; plant roots in a container have less protection than they do when they are buried in the ground.

ABOVE: **Plant up a hanging basket to cheer the winter months; this one includes colorful pansies, ivy, and skimmia.**

LAWNS AND WATER GARDENS
GENERAL TASKS

As long as the weather has not been too dry, lawns should still be looking good. Next month is the best time to start a new lawn from seed—prepare the ground for it now. Water gardens should also be in good condition, with plenty of color and interest from both floating plants and marginals.

Keeping ponds healthy

Now that floating plants such as nymphaea (water lilies) have spread their leaves to shade much of the water surface from direct sun, any problems with green water owing to algae that occurred earlier in the summer should be over. Lilies and similar plants should still have plenty of flowers to add color to the water garden scene, but some of the older leaves will be yellowing and starting to die back. Remove these from the water as soon as you notice them; it is important to keep decaying plant refuse out of the pond as far as possible. Also continue to check the undersides of lily leaves

RIGHT: **Waterfalls not only look and sound attractive, they can help to keep the water in a pool well aerated —often vital in thundery weather.**

for the transparent blobs of snails' eggs, and remove any found. Water snails can be a serious plant pest, and snails or eggs are often introduced unwittingly when new plants are bought. The ramshorn snail is the only satisfactory species for garden pools.

Aerate pond water

Normally, the water in a pond takes in oxygen and releases carbon dioxide at the surface, but in sultry, thundery weather this process becomes very slow or may stop altogether. Fish in the pool can be badly affected, and can sometimes be seen at the surface of the pool gulping in air: if nothing is done they may die. The effect is worst at night, when pond plants are adding to the carbon dioxide content of the water.

The simple remedy is to stir up the water to increase its surface area and allow some of the carbon dioxide to escape. This can be done by leaving fountains or waterfalls running, by stirring the water vigorously with a stick or aiming a forceful jet from a hose into the pool.

Prepare sites for sowing grass

Early fall is the best time to sow seed for a new lawn, but now is the time to start preparing the soil. Remember that the grass is going to be a permanent feature for years to come, so it is well worth making sure that the basic preparation is thorough. This is your only chance to get soil conditions right.

1 Clear the site of existing turf, cultivated trees, shrubs, and plants and weeds. It is especially important to get rid of perennial weeds because they will be very difficult to control once the lawn is established. Use a weedkiller such as glyphosate carefully where necessary.

2 Once the site is cleared of plant growth, remove any other obstructions there may be, such as large stones, paving slabs and so on (right). The cleared site can then be leveled, filling in dips and flattening humps.

3 If the site slopes steeply it may be necessary to reduce the gradient or construct terraces. Where this sort of work is essential, remove the topsoil and stack it nearby, adjusting the levels by moving subsoil. Re-spread the topsoil evenly over the leveled base once the work is completed.

4 Check the structure and condition of the soil. Add well-rotted organic matter such as garden mix to improve heavy and light soils. Give it a final once-over before sowing (left).

Preparing for a new lawn

Turf is the quickest way to make a new lawn, giving virtually instant results. Although soil preparation for turf does not need to be quite as painstaking as for seed sowing, it is still worth cultivating the area to be turfed thoroughly well in advance, removing perennial weeds, stones etc. and adding a long-lasting fertilizer to get the grass off to a good start.

LEFT: A well-established, well-kept lawn sets off the whole of the rest of the garden. It will soon be time to start making new lawns.

KITCHEN GARDEN
SOWING AND PLANTING

The reward for all your work in the vegetable garden becomes apparent as more and more crops are ready to harvest. It's still time to be thinking ahead, however; there are crops to be sown or planted now for next season, and winter crops to look after for the more immediate future.

Spinach for spring

The tender green leaves of spinach make a very welcome vegetable in the spring, and plants sown now are less likely to run to seed than crops sown in the spring for summer use. Traditionally, prickly-seeded varieties of spinach are the ones to sow in late summer and early fall, using round-seeded types in spring. However, nowadays many modern hybrids are equally good for both seasons.

Sow seeds thinly in drills about 12in/30cm apart; water the soil the day before if conditions are dry. Once the seedlings emerge, thin them to around 9in/23cm. Depending on the

RIGHT: **Sow plenty of rows of spinach. The leaves shrink so much when they are cooked that you always need more than you think you will.**

weather, there may be leaves to harvest from late fall right through the winter, but the most reliable flush of foliage will be in early spring. Earlier cropping can be obtained if the seedlings are covered with cloches.

Japanese onions

Onion varieties such as "Express Yellow" and "Senshyu Semi-globe Yellow" are specially bred for sowing in late summer. They are winter hardy, and will give the earliest crop next year in early to midsummer. The timing of sowing is fairly critical, however. Plants that are sown too soon often run to seed prematurely in the spring, whereas those that

are sown too late either give a disappointing crop of small bulbs or die out over winter. Gardeners in cold districts need to sow one or two weeks ahead of those in milder areas. Sow in rows 9–12in/23–30cm apart, and leave the seedlings until spring before thinning them to 4in/10cm apart. Water the drills before sowing, and damp them down frequently in the days following if the weather is hot, to cool the soil and improve germination.

Plant strawberries

The yield and quality of strawberries usually drops off after three years of cropping, and it is advisable to think about replacing the bed with new plants after this time. Replacing one-third of the plants in the strawberry bed each year means that you will continue to have strawberries to harvest every year.

1 Strawberry plants are prone to a number of virus diseases that reduce their yields, and it is a good idea to buy certified virus-free stock to give them the best possible start.

2 Prepare the soil well before obtaining the plants, adding well-rotted organic matter and clearing away all traces of weeds, so difficult to control in any well-established strawberry bed.

3 Well-rooted runners in small pots or peat blocks can be bought from garden centers, or by mail order from specialist suppliers. They should be planted as soon as possible after arrival, spacing them around 12–18in/30–45cm apart in rows 3ft/90cm apart. Arrange them in their pots to your satisfaction (below).

4 Plant with a trowel (above), firming the plants in thoroughly with the sole of your boot. The crown of the plant should be just level with the soil surface. Water after planting, using a medium fine spray on the watering can or hose nozzle to avoid disturbing or flooding the roots (below).

LEFT: **Crops for harvesting in winter, such as cabbages, should be coming along strongly. Keep them weed-free, and water them in dry weather.**

KITCHEN GARDEN
GATHERING THE HARVEST

In late summer and early fall crops are ripening daily, and much of the produce may go to waste unless it is picked regularly and stored correctly. Some crops need to be consumed as soon as possible after picking, but others will keep for some time as long as the right storage method is used.

Harvesting and storing produce

The best time for harvesting is early in the day, before crops lose their moisture in the warm weather. Handle the produce carefully so that it is not bruised; any damaged crops should be put to one side for immediate consumption.

Once picked, keep fruit or vegetables intended for short-term storage in a cool, dark place; the salad box of a refrigerator is usually ideal if there is room.

Root vegetables can be left in the ground over the winter, or stored in boxes of almost-dry mix or in paper sacks. Dense-hearted cabbages, ripe marrows, and pumpkins, and many varieties of apples and pears will keep well in a cool, airy shed; onions and shallots can be plaited into ropes or stored in trays somewhere dry. Don't forget to make jelly and pickles, as these are good, traditional preservation methods for a wide range of fruit and vegetables.

BELOW: **Gooseberries for cooking are picked as soon as they are large enough. Dessert varieties, for eating raw, must be left on the bushes to ripen.**

Freezing

Freezing is probably the most popular method of long-term storage, and is appropriate for soft fruit, or any crop that deteriorates quickly once picked. It preserves the color and flavor of the fruit well, though the texture may suffer in some cases.

Pick over the fruit well; wash it only if essential. It can be open-frozen (i.e. spread on trays), frozen in containers packed with dry sugar, or frozen in sugar syrup—whichever is most appropriate. Fruit normally cooked (cooking apples and gooseberries, for example) can be cooked before freezing. Remember to label the packs because fruit is difficult to identify once frozen.

Most well prepared fruit will keep in excellent condition for over a year in the freezer.

Pruning fruit in summer

Apples and other fruits grown as cordons, fans or espaliers need pruning in the summer to control their growth. Correct pruning is a vital technique for keeping these forms under control so that the plants remain both attractive and fruitful.

1 Summer pruning should be carried out over a number of weeks as the shoots reach the correct stage. Shoots that are ready for pruning are about pencil thickness, and becoming woody and dark in color at their base (above).

2 The first leaves from the base on each shoot are known as the basal cluster and usually consist of three leaves growing in the same plane. This basal cluster is ignored when counting the number of leaves on the shoot (above).

BELOW: **Pick early-maturing varieties of apple as soon as they separate easily from the tree.**

3 The severity of pruning depends on the type of shoot. New lateral shoots that are more than 8in/20cm long, and growing from the main stem, are cut back to three leaves above the basal cluster. Cut just above the bud in the leaf axil, angling the cut slightly so that it slopes away from the bud (above).

4 Side-shoots that are growing from existing laterals or fruit-bearing spurs should be cut back harder, reducing them to just one leaf above the basal cluster. This pruning system improves the cropping potential of the tree by encouraging the development of fruiting spurs, and checking excessive leafy shoot growth and production (above).

SUMMER
TASKS & PLANT OVERVIEW

Early summer tasks

ORNAMENTAL GARDEN
• Plant out tender bedding and sow biennials and perennials
• Prune spring-flowering shrubs and trim hedges
• Trim alpines after flowering
• Tie climbers to their supports; increase them by layering
• Tie in border plants and apply a liquid feed; dead-head as appropriate
• Cut down euphorbias that are past their best
• Treat pests as they appear
• Divide and replant flag irises and primulas (primroses) after flowering
• Take cuttings of dianthus (pinks)
• Feed and water plants in containers
• Spray roses against pests and diseases if needed. Remove suckers
• Lift and divide narcissus (daffodils)
• Mulch borders to keep down weeds
• Look out for fall-flowering bulbs and Madonna lilies *Lilium candidum* and plant as early as possible

LAWNS
• Continue regular mowing and watering, weeding and feeding lawns as necessary
• Mow areas of naturalized bulbs
• Deal with moles as molehills appear

KITCHEN GARDEN
• Continue weeding and watering as necessary
• Earth up potatoes and lift early varieties
• Sow late crops such as radishes, summer spinach, lettuces, and turnips
• Continue planting out pole and bush beans, leeks, and winter brassicas
• Pinch out beans and harvest early peas
• Plant out tomatoes and peppers
• Control cabbage white caterpillars
• Remove runners from strawberries
• Thin young tree fruits
• Summer prune red and white currants, gooseberries

Midsummer tasks

GENERAL
• Check plants for pests and diseases
• Continue watering
• Install garden lighting

ORNAMENTAL GARDEN
• Prune shrubs that have finished flowering as necessary; prune wisteria
• Continue trimming hedges
• Prick out perennials and biennials sown earlier
• Dead-head flowers and cut back rock plants that are becoming untidy
• Start to take cuttings of shrubs
• Cut back early-flowering border plants to encourage a second flush
• Dead-head, prune, and water plants in containers
• Cut flowers for use indoors
• Stake and tie dahlias; disbud them if large blooms are required
• Check *Aster novi-belgii* (Michaelmas daisies) for mildew, and treat if needed
• Order spring bulbs

LAWNS
• Leave clippings on the grass sometimes
• Increase mowing height in dry weather

WATER GARDEN
• Top up ponds with fresh water
• Continue to feed fish to help build them up for winter

KITCHEN GARDEN
• Harvest vegetables regularly as ready
• Check potatoes for potato blight
• Pick herbs for drying, freezing and use
• Thin seedlings
• Continue planting winter vegetables
• Water pole beans when flowering
• Remove straw on strawberry beds after fruiting, and cut the foliage from strawberries not required for propagation. Root strawberry runners
• Cut off foliage affected by silver leaf on plums and other stone fruit
• Start summer-pruning of trained apples and pears
• Cut down summer-fruiting raspberry canes after fruiting

Late summer tasks

ORNAMENTAL GARDEN
• Remove dead flowers from lavender and thyme, and clip plants
• Take cuttings of tender and dubiously hardy perennials to overwinter
• Weed borders and tidy up the plants
• Feed late-flowering border plants
• Check dahlias and chrysanthemums for earwig damage
• Pot up mint for winter use
• Trim back border plants to allow late-flowering varieties to be seen
• Order bare-root shrubs and trees for fall planting
• Plant container-grown shrubs and border plants
• Clear out faded window boxes and hanging baskets, and replant them for winter interest
• Trim evergreen hedges for last time
• Remove annuals that have finished flowering
• Continue to take semi-ripe cuttings of shrubs

LAWNS
• Prepare the site for sowing grass

WATER GARDEN
• Aerate ponds in sultry weather

KITCHEN GARDEN
• Plant strawberries
• Summer-prune trained fruit
• Pick early apples as they ripen
• Continue to harvest vegetables and soft fruit, freezing or storing gluts for later use
• Feed outdoor tomatoes with high-potash fertilizer; remove yellowed lower leaves
• Blanch leeks by drawing up soil around the stems
• Sow prickly-seeded spinach or spinach beet for a spring crop
• Thin out new summer-fruiting raspberry canes
• Pick fall-fruiting raspberries
• Provide marrows and pumpkins with straw to keep fruits off wet soil
• Ripen onions by bending their necks

Ornamental plants in season

Early summer

TREES AND SHRUBS

Abelia x grandiflora
Buddleja globosa
Buddleja alternifolia
Ceanothus (Californian lilac)
Cistus purpureus (rock rose)
Deutzia gracilis
Escallonia
Lonicera periclymenum (common honeysuckle)
Philadelphus (mock orange)
Potentilla (cinquefoil)
Pyracantha (firethorn)
Rhododendron
Rosa (rose)
Spiraea douglasii
Syringa (lilac)
Viburnum plicatum (japanese snowball bush)
Weigela
Wisteria sinensis (Chinese wisteria)

PERENNIALS AND BEDDING PLANTS

Achillea filipendulina "Gold Plate" (yarrow)
Ageratum (floss flower)
Althaea
Aquilegia vulgaris (granny's bonnet)
Astrantia major (Hattie's pincushion)
Campanula (bellflower)
Coreopsis (tickseed)
Delphinium elatum hybrids
Dianthus (carnation, pink)
Dictamnus albas (burning bush)
Digitalis purpurea (common foxglove)
Fuchsia (bedding varieties)
Geranium
Heuchera (coral flower)
Iris
Lobelia erinus
Lupinus (lupin)
Nepeta x faassenii
Paeonia (peony)
Papaver orientale (oriental poppy)
Pelargonium

BULBS

Allium (onion)
Camassia leichtlinii, C. quamash (quamash)
Iris
Lilium (lily)

Midsummer

TREES AND SHRUBS

Abelia floribunda, A. x grandiflora
Catalpa bignonioides (Indian bean tree)
Ceanothus (Californian lilac)
Cistus (rock rose)
Clethra alnifolia (sweet pepper bush)
Cytisus battandieri (pineapple bloom)
Escallonia
Eucryphia
Fuchsia magellanica
Genista (broom)
Helianthemum (rock rose)
Hydrangea macrophylla
Hypericum calycinum (Aaron's beard)
Lavandula (lavender)
Lonicera periclymenum (common honeysuckle)
Olearia x haastii (daisy bush)
Philadelphus (mock orange)
Rosa (rose)
Vinca major (greater periwinkle), V. minor (lesser periwinkle)

PLANTS WITH SCENTED FLOWERS

Achillea
Alstroemeria (Peruvian lily)
Althaea
Astilbe
Astrantia major (Hattie's pincushion)
Begonia semperflorens
Campanula (bellflower)
Chrysanthemum maximum
Coreopsis (tickseed)
Delphinium elatum hybrids
Dianthus (carnation, pink)
Digitalis purpurea (common foxglove)
Echinops ritro (globe thistle)
Erigeron (fleabane)
Fuchsia
Gaillardia x grandiflora
Geranium
Geum (avens)
Gypsophila paniculata
Helenium
Hemerocallis (day lily)
Heuchera (coral flower)
Kniphofia (red hot poker)
Lathyrus (everlasting pea)
Lupinus (lupin)
Nepeta x faassenii (catmint)
Nicotiana alata (tobacco plant)
Oenothera (evening primrose)
Pelargonium
Penstemon
Phlox paniculata (perennial phlox)
Romneya coulteri (tree poppy)
Scabiosa caucasica (pincushion flower)
Solidago (Aaron's rod)

BULBS

Cardiocrinum giganteum
Crocosmia x crocosmiiflora
Eucomis bicolor (pineapple flower)
Gladiolus
Lilium (lily)

Late summer

TREES AND SHRUBS

Buddleja davidii
Campsis radicans (trumpet creeper)
Clerodenrum bungei
Eucryphia
Fuchsia
Hebe
Hibiscus syriacus
Hydrangea macrophylla
Hypericum (St John's Wort)
Lonicera (honeysuckle)
Rosa (rose)

PERENNIALS

Acanthus (bear's breeches)
Achillea (yarrow)
Aconitum (aconite)
Anemone hybrida
Aster
Begonia semperflorens
Chrysanthemum
Gazania
Helenium
Helianthus annuus (sunflower)
Hemerocallis (day lily)
Kniphofia (red hot poker)
Phlox paniculata (perennial phlox)
Romneya coulteri (tree poppy)
Rudbeckia (coneflower)

BULBS

Crocosmia x crocosmiiflora
Cyclamen purpurascens
Eucomis bicolor (pineapple flower)
Gladiolus hybrids
Lilium (lily)

LEFT: **There should still be plenty of color from the flower borders for some weeks to come. Dead-heading prolongs the flowering period.**

EARLY FALL

 Many of the early fall tasks involve clearing away the debris of the summer season, but there's also plenty of sowing and planting to do. Warm, sunny days and an abundance of bright flowers, foliage, and fruits make the melancholy job of tidying up a much more pleasant affair.

Although fall marks the end of the main growing season, it is a busy time in the garden. There are crops to be gathered, leaves to sweep up and tender plants to be protected before the first frost arrives. Misty mornings, heavy dew, and cool weather combine to make ideal conditions for fungus diseases; regular checks and prompt treatment are necessary to prevent plant losses.

The dying leaves of deciduous trees and shrubs often make a remarkable display of brilliant color, but all too soon the show is ended by gales which bring the leaves tumbling down. Dead leaves must be removed from garden ponds, lawns, alpine plants, paths, and patios before they can do damage or become a nuisance, and leaf clearing can be a major job in large gardens.

Beds and borders should still be putting on a show with late-blooming plants if varieties have been chosen wisely. Tidy spent border plants and old stems to show off these late-flowering plants to advantage. Weeds continue to thrive and need removing regularly.

Fall is an excellent time for planting both bare-root and container-grown plants. It is also time to plant spring bulbs, always a pleasant task, as we can look forward

ABOVE: **Plants such as the architectural, steely-blue eryngium continue to make a bold display well into the fall months.**

to their flowers signaling that winter is over in a few months' time.

There are seeds to be sown in early fall, too. Some hardy annuals will brave the winter cold and produce early flowers next summer if sown outdoors now. In the vegetable garden, peas and beans can be tried, and fall is the perfect time to sow a new lawn.

ORNAMENTAL GARDEN
GENERAL TASKS

Even when late flowers have faded, the fall garden need never be dull. Deciduous foliage can provide some spectacularly brilliant colors; berry-bearing plants continue the show for months, provided birds don't eat the lot. Evergreen plants also start to come into their own in the fall.

Enjoy fall color

Shortening day length triggers off brilliant reds, oranges, and yellows in some deciduous leaves. Plants vary in the intensity of color produced. Acer (maple), berberis (barberry), cercidiphyllum, fothergilla, nyssa (tulepo), parthenocissus (virginia creeper), hamamelis (witch hazel) and many others provide some reliably bright and colorful species and varieties.

Climate and soil conditions have a major part to play, too. The more marked the contrast between day and night temperatures, the better the leaf color. Wet, mild weather, when the leaves tend to remain green and hang on the trees for longer, can also spoil the show. But other factors are more within our control. Prevent fall leaves from being prematurely blown from trees by planting them in a sheltered position. Provide fertilizers during the growing season to promote plenty of lush leaf growth to turn color later. For lime-hating plants, acid (rather than neutral) soil greatly intensifies their leaf color.

BELOW: **Fall color from deciduous trees and shrubs can make a brilliant spectacle. Select varieties specially bred for their colorful foliage.**

Protect berries from birds

Bunches of brightly colored berries can decorate the garden right through fall and winter, but often the first sharp frost brings flocks of birds to strip the berries from the plants. Netting (provided it is supported away from the plants to prevent birds pecking through it) protects the berries but usually spoils the appearance of the plants. Bird-deterrent sprays are an alternative; they use a harmless but bitter-tasting compound to make berries unpalatable. Yellow and orange berries are far less likely to be attacked than bright red ones, so try planting varieties such as *Pyracantha* "Orange Glow" and *Ilex aquifolium* "Bacciflava."

Protect non-hardy plants

A number of garden and patio plants are not reliably hardy in many gardens and need a little help to survive the winter. If you have taken cuttings from these in late summer (see page 81) you will at least have some plants in reserve in case the worst happens.

1 Herbaceous plants die down in fall and spend the winter below soil as a dormant rootstock. Tender plants may not survive frost and cold penetrating the ground, but an insulating mulch of dry leaves, dead bracken or chipped bark heaped over the root area will help them survive.

2 Small trees and shrubs can be protected from low temperature damage by surrounding them with insulating material such as straw or bracken. The material must be dry to avoid fungus disease, and it must be loosely packed so that air can circulate through it.

3 Surround the shrub with a circle of wire netting supported on stakes, and loosely pack the wire cage with the insulating material. A large piece of plastic sheeting placed over the top will keep the material dry (above).

4 The roots of plants in containers are particularly prone to cold weather damage. Lag the container with straw or a similar material; bubble wrap sheeting is useful for wrapping around tubs and pots in a double layer (above).

Take cuttings of evergreens

Shoots to be used as cuttings should have ripened at the base and be around 6in/15cm long. Pull them away from the main stem with a small heel of bark at the base; treat them with a rooting hormone combined with a fungicide to prevent rotting, and insert them into trays of sandy sowing and cuttings mix. Overwinter the cuttings in a cold frame or unheated greenhouse; they should have rooted by the following spring.

ORNAMENTAL GARDEN
PLANTING AND SOWING

It's time to prepare for a colorful spring, by replacing summer bedding plants and annuals that are past their best, and by planting spring-flowering bulbs in lawns. New evergreen shrubs can also be planted safely now, as long as they are not likely to be damaged by cold winter weather.

Plant hardy evergreens

Because evergreen plants carry their full complement of leaves at planting time, extra care must be taken to protect them from adverse weather. Strong winds carry moisture away from the leaf surfaces, leading to scorching and leaf fall, and leaf tips and margins can be damaged by hard frosts. Make sure that evergreens planted now are quite hardy; more tender types will do better if they are planted in late spring.

Prepare the soil for evergreens in the normal way, digging deeply and adding some slow-release fertilizer such as bonemeal to the base of the planting hole. Make sure you firm in plants thoroughly; because they have leaves to catch the wind, root rock can be a problem. They should also be firmed back in thoroughly with the ball of your foot after windy or frosty weather.

If cold, windy weather strikes soon after planting evergreens, protect them with a windbreak while they get established (see page 110).

BELOW: **Evergreen shrubs and trees really come into their own during the fall and winter months, providing color and interesting shapes.**

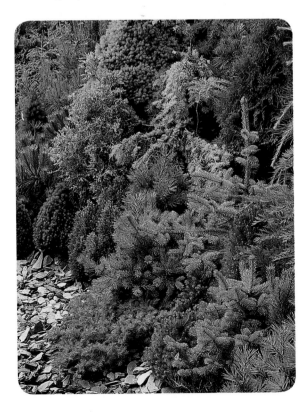

Replace summer bedding

Summer bedding and annual flowers will soon be past their best. Over the next few weeks it's time to replace them with spring bedding for some early interest next year.

Put spent plants on the compost pile. Dig the vacant soil over well, removing weeds, and add some slow-release fertilizer: refill containers with fresh potting mix. Plant up beds and containers with spring bedding plants such as myosotis (forget-me-not), viola (pansies), primula (primroses), and erysimum (wallflowers), interplanted with spring bulbs such as tulips and hyacinths for an effective display.

Naturalizing spring bulbs

Bulbs growing through grass always look particularly attractive during the spring flowering season. Daffodils and crocus are the two subjects most popular for growing like this, but several others are also successful, including colchicum (fall crocus), *Fritillaria meleagris* (snakeshead fritillary), muscari (grape hyacinth), and scilla (squill).

1 Informality is the key to success when naturalizing bulbs. To look as natural as possible, handfuls of the bulbs are scattered randomly over the area, and planted as they fall, with one or two minor adjustments (left).

2 Removing plugs of turf and soil to plant the bulbs individually is hard work (right). The lawn area should be watered deeply two or three days before planting to soften the turf; a long-handled bulb planter makes the job much easier.

3 Drop a bulb at the base of the hole and replace the soil plug, treading it down lightly. Make sure the bottom of the bulb is in firm contact with the soil at the base of the hole, not wedged halfway up.

4 When planting small bulbs such as crocus it is often easier to fold back a section of turf and plant direct into the soil below. Cut an H-shape with an edging iron (left), undercut and fold back the two flaps of turf. Plant the bulbs randomly into the soil (right), water, then fold the flaps back into place and firm thoroughly.

5 Before planting bulbs in lawns, remember that the grass cannot be mown in spring until the bulb leaves have died. Choose an informal area of the garden where this will not matter.

EARLY FALL

LAWNS AND WATER GARDENS
GENERAL TASKS

Mild, damp fall weather encourages toadstools—an unwelcome sight in the middle of the lawn—but is ideal for the germination of grass seed. Garden ponds need care now to prevent the water from being polluted with decaying plant matter, and pond fish need help to face the winter ahead.

Remove tender pond plants

Some floating pond plants make an attractive contribution to the pool in the summer, but will not survive a cold winter out of doors. They include the water hyacinth (*Eichhornia crassipes*) and the water lettuce (*Pistia stratioides*). Remove them from the pond well before the first frosts are due. Overwinter them in a frost-free greenhouse, placed in a washing-up bowl or similar container filled with pond water, with a lining of mud at the bottom. Put them back in the pond in early summer. *Trapa natans* (water chestnut) is also frost tender but is an annual that will not survive the winter anyway. It should also be removed from the pond to prevent the decaying foliage from polluting the water.

Net ponds against falling leaves

It is vital to keep fall leaves out of the pond. Decaying plant material gives off toxic gases which will poison fish and turn the water stagnant. Use fine mesh plastic netting to cover the surface of the pond, ensuring that it is pegged down securely all around the edges.

Before putting the net in position, cut down excess growth of oxygenating plants and remove this, together with all dead and dying foliage and flowers from water and marginal plants.

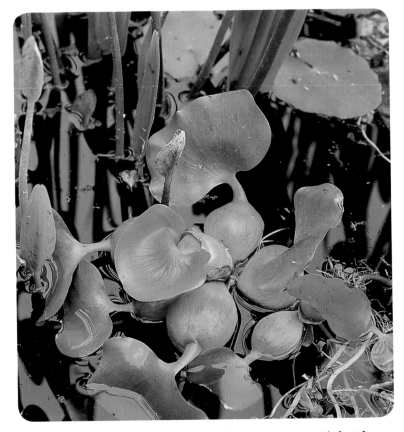

ABOVE: **The water hyacinth (*Eichhornia crassipes*) is a serious invasive pest in frost-free areas, but is killed off in fall in cold climates.**

Sow a new lawn

Seed is the cheapest way of making a new lawn, and allows most control over which grass varieties are used. Although lawn seed can also be sown successfully in spring, the best time for the job is early fall, while the soil is still warm and the conditions are moist.

1 Give the prepared site a final raking to level it and break down the clods of soil to a fine, even, crumbly texture (right). If the soil is loose and puffy, shuffle over the whole site to firm it gently with your feet before raking.

2 Weigh out the correct quantity of seed for the area to be sown (sowing rates should be given on the packs, and are usually about 1–1½ oz per sq yd/35–50g per sq m). Split the total quantity of seed into two.

3 Sow the first half of the seed mixture over the whole lawn as evenly as possible, working from top to bottom; then sow the second half working from side to side (above). This double sowing helps to even out any inconsistencies in the sowing rate.

4 Use a spring-tine rake to scratch the seed lightly into the soil but do not try to bury it (below). Using seed treated with a bird repellent will cut down the bird nuisance; if necessary, the lawn area can be protected with plastic netting supported on stakes.

Remove toadstools from lawns

Crops of toadstools are common on turf at this time of year, appearing magically overnight. There are many different types of fungi. Most of them grow on organic matter in the soil and are quite harmless. If their appearance spoils the look of the lawn, they can simply be picked off and thrown away—they appear for only a short time each year.

One type that is more serious is *Marasmius oreades* (fairy ring fungus) that can cause obvious, unsightly green rings in the grass. Although various fungicides may be suggested, this fungus is almost impossible to treat successfully; remaking the lawn may be the only answer. The deep green rings may be disguised by treating the lawn with fertilizer to green up the rest of the grass.

KITCHEN GARDEN
GENERAL TASKS

There are sowings and plantings to be made in the kitchen garden, and harvested crops need to be stored away carefully. Make sure winter vegetables are progressing satisfactorily, and give them the protection they need from the bad weather that may be around the corner.

Harvest pumpkins

Pumpkins and winter squashes should be cut and brought under cover before the first frosts. As long as they are fully ripened, they can be stored for many weeks in a cool but frost-free, dry shed. Check the fruit has no signs of damage or rot before storing, particularly where it has been resting on the soil.

Maincrop potatoes should also be lifted now. On a dry, sunny day, fork the potatoes out of the soil and leave them on the surface of the ground for several hours to dry. Store them in hessian or heavy-duty paper sacks, or wooden or sturdy cardboard boxes. Do not use plastic sacks; they retain moisture and cause rotting. Store in a cool, dark place and cover the potatoes to exclude all light.

BELOW: **Winter squashes should store well for weeks, but any that are damaged should be used up straight away as they will only rot in store.**

Support winter brassicas

Winter brassicas such as broccoli, Brussels sprouts, kale, and various cabbages can make quite tall plants. In exposed gardens they run the risk of being blown over because they have relatively shallow root systems. In windy areas, provide each plant with a sturdy wooden stake. The earliest varieties of Brussels sprouts will now be ready for picking. Start harvesting from the base of the stem, where the largest buttons are, and gradually work upward.

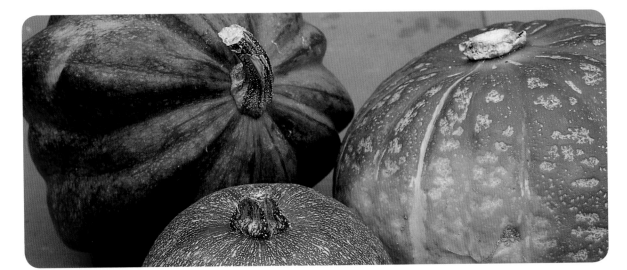

Lift root vegetables

Some root crops will happily stay in the soil right through winter, but others are best lifted at the end of the growing season and stored above ground, especially in areas where the soil is heavy and inclined to remain wet in winter. Wet conditions are likely to cause the roots to rot.

1 Carrots are at their tastiest pulled young (right) and eaten straight away, but maincrop varieties make a useful crop for eating throughout the winter. If left in the soil too long they tend to split, which can make them unusable.

2 Fork up the carrots carefully to avoid spearing them, and shake off loose earth. Cut off the foliage (below), and layer the carrots in boxes of fine, almost dry soil, sand or peat. Store the boxes in a cool, dark place, e.g., shed or garage. Use up any damaged carrots straight away.

4 Beets are lifted and stored in the same way as carrots, but the leafy tops should be twisted off, not cut with a knife, to avoid bleeding. Lift the roots before they become too big because they are inclined to go woody (below).

3 Beets are often pickled in vinegar, but it is also delicious if cooked and eaten like any other fresh root vegetable. The golden variety will not stain pink any other food with which it comes into contact, as the standard red varieties do.

Protect summer-planted potatoes

If you planted a few cold-stored potatoes in summer to give you new potatoes in the fall and winter, it will soon be time to protect the plants from cold weather, depending on the climate in your area. Use a mulch of straw, dry bracken or similar material along the rows. The first tubers may be ready for harvesting in mid-fall, but in reasonable conditions can be kept in the ground until mid or late winter.

KITCHEN GARDEN
PLANTING AND SOWING

As well as harvesting the abundance of crops in the kitchen garden now, keep some continuity of cropping going with further plantings and sowings. A little extra protection from the weather can be gained by sowing under cover. Seedlings from earlier sowings need thinning out or transplanting.

Plant onion sets

Onion sets planted in the fall will give an early crop next year, several weeks before maincrop varieties are ready for harvest. Varieties available for fall planting have been chosen for their hardiness and disease resistance, and include "Early Yellow Globe," "Yellow Spanish," "Snow White hybrid," and the red-fleshed "Red Hamburger."

Prepare the soil thoroughly and mix in some coarse sand or grit to lighten it if necessary, as fall-planted sets need free-draining conditions. Plant the sets in rows 14in/35cm apart, spacing the sets 4–6in/10–15cm apart in the row. Always plant onion sets with a trowel, because simply pushing the sets into the soil can compact the ground immediately beneath them, making it difficult for the roots to penetrate. Fall-planted onions can be ready to harvest as early as late spring, but they can be stored for only a few weeks.

BELOW: Fall-planted onion sets should produce a crop that is ready for harvesting very early the following summer.

Thin out seedlings

Seedlings from late sown crops, including lettuce, radish, spinach, and turnips, among others, should be thinned out as soon as they are large enough. This thinning is best carried out in progressive stages to allow for plant losses—thin to half the final recommended spacing first, then remove every other plant later on, as necessary.

Where seedlings are very crowded, great care is necessary to avoid disturbing the roots of the plants which are to remain after thinning. If the weather is dry, water the row of seedlings before thinning to make it easier to tease away the unwanted plants.

Lettuce for winter

It's great to have been able to cut fresh salads straight from the garden through the summer, and it's something that will be sadly missed over the next few months. However, it is possible to have a supply of winter lettuce from the greenhouse—the plants won't be as succulent and full-hearted as summer varieties, but they're still worth growing. Sow the seed now; once the seedlings are large enough, they can be transplanted into growing bags, or direct into the greenhouse border.

1 It's important to choose the right variety of lettuce for growing in the greenhouse in winter because only a few are suitable for this method. Check with your local garden center to see what is the best choice.

2 An unheated greenhouse is quite suitable for growing winter lettuce, although heated greenhouses will give a faster-maturing crop. Cold frames and polytunnels can also be used successfully for growing winter salads.

3 Sow the seed thinly on a prepared seedtray of moist soil mix and cover lightly (above). Lettuce seed becomes dormant in very hot conditions, so it is important to keep the tray in a well-ventilated, lightly shaded position after sowing.

4 Once the seedlings are showing through, move the tray to full light. Water very carefully to avoid fungus disease. Prick out the seedlings to wider spacings as soon as they are large and strong enough to be handled easily (above).

RIGHT: Transplant cabbages to their cropping positions. If preferred, space the young plants closely to obtain "greens" rather than densely hearted cabbages.

MID-FALL

 The tidy-up continues as more and more leaves hit the ground and late season flowers fade. As the weather becomes increasingly cold, it's time to protect the more delicate plants. Remain on the alert for frosts, though with luck you may be enjoying a warm, sunny Indian summer.

This is often the time when fall leaf color is at its glorious best, but it won't be long before a windy spell brings the leaves to the ground in drifts. Fallen leaves are not so bad when they are dry and crisp, but once rain turns them to a slimy brown sludge they pose a danger to both plants and people. Remove them from lawns and small, vulnerable plants like alpines before the leaves smother them; also clear them from paths and steps before somebody slips in the mush and injures themselves.

Cut down spent flowers and dying foliage in herbaceous borders, but don't be too enthusiastic. Some dead, brown stems and leaves have an architectural value, and seedheads can be particularly decorative.

At what time the first frost arrives, and just how bad the weather might be, depends largely on your particular location. Some regions can rely on mild falls and winters, while others can guarantee that freezing conditions will arrive in the near future. Only experience can tell you what to expect, but always be prepared for the worst. Better to prepare your dubiously hardy plants for icy weather that does not arrive, than leave them to be killed by a single unexpected cold snap.

ABOVE: **The red rose hips of *Rosa glauca*, usually grown for its purple foliage.** OPPOSITE: **The vigorous climber *Parthenocissus quinquefolia*, commonly known as Virginia creeper, has outstanding fall foliage.**

As more plants in the kitchen garden finish cropping and are removed, vacant soil begins to appear, ready to be dug over for next spring. If the fall weather is too depressing, cheer yourself up by continuing to plant spring-flowering bulbs and spring bedding to give you something to look forward to at the end of the winter.

MID-FALL
GENERAL TASKS

Clean up fall leaves and plant remains and transform them into valuable compost and leaf mold for the garden. A number of garden plants need protection from fall and winter weather now. It is not just cold that is the problem; excess rain can have serious effects, too.

Cold protection for plants

Continue to provide protection for plants that may not be reliably hardy in your area (see page 95). It is often difficult to know just how well a particular plant will survive local conditions, but any plant that is described as "rather tender," "dubiously hardy," "half-hardy," or "suitable for favored areas" should be given extra care in regions where there are penetrating frosts. This is particularly important for young plants, or recently planted subjects that have not had a chance to establish properly and become acclimatized to the conditions. Plants such as agapanthus (African blue lily), cordyline (cabbage palm), phygelius, yucca, eucalyptus, passiflora (passion flower), and acacia (wattle) are among many that may need protection.

Remember that many plants that will happily survive overnight frosts where the temperature rises during the day are likely to be killed by cold spells where freezing conditions persist for several days at a time.

Keep off excess rain

It is often excessively wet rather than cold conditions that kill plants during the fall and winter. Plants with furry leaves, such as verbascum, are particularly prone to rotting in wet weather because the fur on the foliage holds on to moisture. Silver-leaved plants are also at risk; they are adapted to dry growing conditions and are often badly affected by a damp atmosphere.

Susceptible plants can usually be protected by covering them with an open-ended cloche, which keeps water off the foliage but still allows air to circulate to help prevent fungus disease from developing.

How to build a compost pile

Virtually all types of soil benefit from the addition of plenty of rotted organic matter, but the problem is usually finding a handy supply of suitable material. Composting your garden refuse has two benefits—it provides a convenient and valuable supply of the organic matter your soil needs, and is also a means of disposing of awkward, bulky waste.

1 A compost pile is simply somewhere where waste material can be gathered together to rot down (right). Confining it within a wire, plastic or wooden bin (it can be either a proprietary composter or a home-made affair) keeps it neat, and helps to encourage rapid decomposition by providing the most favorable conditions.

2 Anything organic (i.e. anything that has once lived) can be composted, but avoid animal products and cooked items because these attract vermin. Young weeds, plant refuse, fruit and vegetable peelings are all suitable. Lawn mowings can be added to the pile if they are well mixed with bulkier, more open waste. Add a layer of garden soil to the pile every so often.

3 Once the bin is full, cover the top with a piece of old carpet or cardboard to keep in the heat and keep out excess rain, and allow the contents to decompose to a dark brown, crumbly, sweet-smelling mass (left). Occasionally turning the sides of the pile to the middle is hard work, but it does speed up the rotting process.

4 The traditional fall bonfire is a wasteful and polluting affair, but can be used for woody prunings and other material that is too hard or bulky to rot down. Diseased plant material and seeding weeds are also best burned rather than composted, as disease spores and weed seeds may not always be killed by the composting process.

Sweep fallen leaves from paths

It is surprising how quickly fallen leaves become slippery when they have been lying around in damp weather. On patios, paths and particularly on steps they can pose a real danger to pedestrians. Sweep them up regularly; apart from anything else, they are easier to gather up when they are still dry. Pack the leaves into plastic sacks, tie the tops and pierce some holes in the sides of the sack with a garden fork. Leave the sacks in a corner of the garden and eventually the contents will rot down into valuable leaf mold.

ORNAMENTAL GARDEN
GENERAL TASKS

Even though the summer is over, the ornamental garden still contains plenty of interest for the weeks ahead. Some plants need to be lifted now and stored under cover for the winter. Flower borders can be tidied, and many perennials can be given a new lease of life by being divided and replanted.

Decorative seedheads

When clearing up the flower border, it's all too easy to cut down plants that have a valuable role in providing fall and winter interest. Many seedheads are highly decorative, and have strong architectural shapes that are very attractive. Don't be too rigorous about dead-heading—leave the final flush of flowers to set seed.

Flowers worth growing for their seedheads include acanthus (bear's breeches), allium, briza (quaking grass), cynara, eryngium (sea holly), festuca (fescue), *Iris foetidissima*, lunaria (honesty), nigella (love-in-a-mist), papaver (poppy), Physalis alkekengi (Chinese lantern), scabious (especially "Paper Moon"), and typha (bullrush). Many border plants also have "everlasting"-type flowerheads that are worth preserving when they are dead, including achillea (yarrow), carlina (carline thistle), hydrangea and *Sedum spectabile*. Their russet-brown shades are more subtle than their summer colors, but produce a pleasing effect, especially when lightly iced with frost.

BELOW: *Sedum spectabile* is one of a number of border plants whose dead flowerheads remain attractive through the fall months.

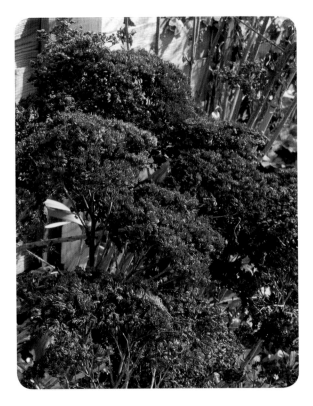

Applying bonemeal

Bonemeal is a natural slow-release fertilizer that gradually supplies its nutrients to the soil. It provides some nitrogen and a much larger proportion of phosphates, and is useful for applying around perennials, trees and shrubs during the dormant season.

Always wear gloves when applying bonemeal. There is a slight risk of the fertilizer being contaminated with animal diseases, particularly anthrax, though this risk is extremely small and should not be a concern provided the bonemeal has been properly sterilized. However, if you have any small cuts or abrasions to your skin, bonemeal—and other powdered fertilizers—will make them sting unpleasantly.

Divide border plants

Division is an easy way to increase your stock of herbaceous perennials. Not only does it give you a new supply of plants, but it actually improves the performance of plants that have been in place for more than a couple of years. Border plants can also be divided in spring, but mid-fall is generally the best time of year to do the job.

1 Popular border plants such as campanula (bell flower), hosta, achillea (yarrow), echinops (globe thistle), and papaver (poppies) are all suitable subjects for division. Dig up the whole clump carefully with a garden fork, and place it on a spare piece of soil or on a plastic sheet on the lawn or path (right).

2 Often the center of the clump will be woody and hard, with the strongest shoots growing around the edge. Splitting the clump up will enable you to discard the unproductive center and rejuvenate the plant by replanting the more vigorous sections.

3 Use two forks back to back to prise tough clumps apart (left), or cut them with a knife. Smaller plants may be teased apart by hand. As a guide, each portion should be large enough to fit comfortably in the palm of the hand, and must have good roots and strong growth buds.

4 Replant the new portions straight away; the roots will dry out if they are exposed to the air for too long. If replanting in the same place, dig the soil over quickly with a trowel, removing any weeds, and incorporate a little bonemeal or similar slow-release fertilizer.

Lift and store dahlias

Dahlias in the border need to be protected from cold, wet winter weather in order to survive until spring. As soon as frosts have blackened the foliage, cut down the main stem to about 6in/15cm and lift the tuberous roots. Store them upside down for a few days in order to allow any moisture to drain from the hollow stems, then clean the soil off the tubers and pack them into trays, covering them with almost-dry soil mix. Store the trays in a cool but frost-free, dry place (such as a garage or shed) over the winter. Gladioli corms and begonia tubers should also be lifted now, and cleaned and stored in boxes of soil mix in a dry, frost-free place, like the dahlias.

MID-FALL

109

ORNAMENTAL GARDEN
PLANTING

Fall is an excellent time for planting, but in windy areas, it is worth providing a temporary windbreak as protection for newly planted subjects. Bulbs pose no such problems. While many spring-flowering types should have been set out last month, there are one or two that prefer later planting.

Bare-root trees and shrubs

Bare-root plants have been lifted from nursery beds in the open ground, and have to be sold in the dormant season when they are more resilient to the disturbance of transplanting. They are usually cheaper than container-grown plants, and there is often a better choice of varieties available. They are also easier to transport than plants in containers, and can be bought by mail order.

Care should be taken not to let the roots dry out any more than is necessary. Try not to expose them to the air but keep them covered by plastic bags, paper or hessian sacks during transportation. Ideally bare-root subjects should be planted immediately, but if that is not possible they can be heeled in to a spare piece of ground temporarily, just covering the roots with fine soil. Inspect the roots immediately before planting, and trim back with secateurs any that show signs of damage.

RIGHT: **Bare-rooted conifers (here wrapped in hessian for transportation) are best transplanted now during the dormant season.**

Protect newly planted shrubs from strong winds

Shrubs that have been planted in exposed positions are at risk of damage from the windy weather that is common at this time of year. Evergreens are most vulnerable because they are still carrying their leaves, but even deciduous plants can be damaged by root rock caused by wind catching the branch framework, or the branches may be snapped off.

Reduce the possibility of damage by erecting a temporary windbreak on the windward side of the shrub. Drive two or three stakes into the ground, and tack windbreak netting, sacking or even old plastic sacks to the stakes to provide shelter. The windbreak can be removed in late spring next year, provided the plants are sufficiently well established.

Plant tulips and hyacinths

Spring bulbs such as narcissus (daffodils) and crocuses should have been planted in early fall, but it pays to wait until now, or even until late fall, before planting tulips and hyacinths. If planted too early they make premature growth that may be damaged by cold weather.

1 Tulips and hyacinths make good subjects for the flower border, especially when mixed with spring bedding plants such as wallflowers and forget-me-nots. Dig the soil deeply and add a slow-release fertilizer such as bonemeal.

2 Dig planting holes with a trowel or use a special bulb planter (right). Make the holes sufficiently deep for the tops of the bulbs to be covered with twice their own depth of soil. This is important, as shallow planting leads to poor flowering.

3 Drop the bulbs into their holes ensuring that they are the correct way up, and that the base of the bulb is in contact with the soil at the bottom of the hole. Return the soil to the hole and cover the bulb, then firm it lightly.

4 Because there will be no sign of the bulbs until next spring, it is easy to forget where they are planted and to damage them by cultivating the ground in winter. Label the area where they are planted to avoid this (left).

LEFT: **Some of the most attractive tulips are the smaller varieties, such as *Tulipa kaufmanniana* hybrids, with their striking, mottled foliage.**

LAWNS AND WATER GARDENS
GENERAL TASKS

Ponds still need attention to ensure that the water is not being polluted by fallen leaves and other plant debris. If you are planning a new lawn, this is an ideal time to lay turf; if you just want to improve the condition of your existing lawn, a bulky top-dressing applied now will work wonders.

Pond plants and marginals

Water gardens can look depressing by this time of year with yellowing foliage and dead flowers of marginals spoiling the pond's appearance. Cut the stems right back to just above water level, taking care not to drop any plant material in the water.

If you have not already cut back underwater oxygenators, do so now. These plants produce rampant growth during the spring and summer, and much of it will die back naturally during the fall and winter.

It is best to anticipate this by using secateurs to reduce the tangle of stems by up to two-thirds. Again, make sure the cut plant material is removed from the water.

Pond fish may still benefit from feeding, depending on the weather and the number of fish in the pool. If it is still relatively warm, try giving a small amount of food to see how interested they are; continue feeding only if they clear up the food given within 5 or 10 minutes.

BELOW: **Tidying pond plants and marginals using secateurs will cut down on the amount of tangled stems when the plants die back now the summer months have ended.**

Remove submersible pond pumps

A submersible pump is the simplest method of powering water garden features such as fountains and waterfalls. If the pump has not already been removed from the water, do so now, cleaning it thoroughly (especially the filter). Store it in a dry place under cover for the winter months.

If it is not convenient to remove the pump—when it is in the center of a large pond and is not easy to reach, for example—it can be left in place, but it should be switched on and run for a short while every few weeks throughout winter, unless the pond is frozen. Removing the pump in fall will help prolong its life, though.

A new lawn from turf

Turf is far more expensive than grass seed but it has one great advantage—it provides an instant effect. It is now easy to obtain special lawn turf made up of fine-leaved grass varieties for high quality, luxury lawns. Meadow turf is cheaper; although the lawn will not be of bowling-green quality it will be adequate for most family gardens. Don't underestimate the amount of work involved in laying turf; it is a hard, heavy job, so round up as much help as you can.

1 Prepare the lawn site in advance, as you would for a new lawn from seed (see page 99). Turf needs to be laid within a day or two of delivery, so make sure you will be able to start laying it straight away.

2 Unfold or unroll the first length of turf and lay it flat on the prepared soil, using a taut line to act as a guide for a straight edge where necessary (right). Use the back of a spade or a special turf beetle to firm down the turf and ensure good contact with the soil.

3 Lay the next length of turf, butting the short edges closely together, and continue like this until the first row is complete (left). Lay the second row tight against the first, staggering the short joints like bricks in a wall. Stand on a plank on the new turf to spread your weight evenly. Continue until the whole area has been covered.

4 Once the turfing is complete, cut the edges of the lawn to shape with a half-moon edging iron, using a taut line (for straight edges) or piece of hosepipe (for curves) as a guide. Trickle a mixture of peat and sand, or some fine soil, into the cracks between the turves to encourage them to knit together (left).

Bulky top-dressing

Mix peat (or peat substitute), good quality, sieved loamy soil and medium horticultural sand (but not yellow builders' sand). The proportions of ingredients depend on the underlying soil type–increase the amount of sand on heavy soils, and use more loam and peat on light soils. Spread the top-dressing all over the grass, working it in between the blades with the back of a rake or a stiff broom. It will make the lawn look very messy to start with but will soon disappear, encouraging strong, dense grass growth next spring and summer.

MID-FALL

KITCHEN GARDEN
GENERAL TASKS

Rhubarb is really a vegetable, although it is always thought of as a fruit. In early spring, tender young rhubarb stems are a real delicacy, and this is the ideal time to plant new crowns. Some soft fruit crops are due for pruning, and hardwood cuttings can be taken to increase or replace stock.

Plant new rhubarb crowns

Rhubarb is best grown from certified virus-free crowns (also known as sets). They are available from good garden centers or by mail order, and consist of a clump of fleshy roots topped by a knobbly crown with one or more large, plump buds. Dig plenty of well-rotted garden compost or manure into the planting site. Do not add any lime because rhubarb prefers slightly acidic soil conditions. Plant the crowns so that the buds are only just covered with soil; if planting more than one crown, set them 3ft/90cm apart. Do not pull too many stems in the spring following planting. "Cherry Red" and "Macdonald" are good varieties. Plant the herb sweet cicely nearby, and include a handful of the foliage when cooking the stems. It reduces the acidity, and you won't need to add so much sugar.

RIGHT: **Rhubarb can be planted at this time of year for harvesting in the early spring. Make sure you grow it from certified virus-free crowns for the best results.**

Winter root crops

Root crops such as parsnips, salsify, and rutabaga can in most areas be left in the ground over winter to be pulled as required, but once the foliage has died down there is nothing to show where they are. Mark the rows clearly now. When you start harvesting, begin at one end of the row and move up the marker to show where you finished lifting the crop, so that you know where to dig next time. In very cold weather, when the soil is frozen, it will be impossible to get at the roots, so some should be lifted and stored in boxes of soil in a shed when an icy spell is forecast.

Take hardwood cuttings of soft fruit

Soft fruit, such as currants and gooseberries, are easy to propagate by hardwood cuttings. The cuttings can be left in the open garden all winter, and need very little skill to root successfully. The most important point to remember is not to insert the cuttings upside down—it's easier than you might think to make a mistake unless you prepare them carefully.

1 Cuttings are taken in the dormant season, using fully ripened wood of the current year's growth. Wait until all the leaves have died before cutting the stems with secateurs. Use strong, healthy stems of pencil thickness.

2 Each stem can be cut into lengths to give several cuttings; it may be easy to forget which end of the cutting is which. Use sharp secateurs to cut stems into 6–10in/15–25cm portions (right), making a straight cut at the base of each length and a sloping cut at the top. Treat the stem bases with rooting hormone.

3 Dig over a suitable piece of moist soil, adding some sharp sand unless it is already free draining. The cuttings will need to be left in place undisturbed for one year. Make a narrow slit trench with a spade, and insert each cutting so that just the top 2in/5cm is visible above ground.

4 Firm the soil back against the cuttings with the ball of your foot, and label the row (left). Apart from occasional weeding, the cuttings need little further attention. Over winter, corky callus tissue forms over the bases of the cuttings, and new roots should grow from this next spring.

Blackcurrants and blackberries

Blackcurrants carry most of next year's crop on the wood that has been produced this season. Cut to the ground all the branches that carried fruit this year, leaving the strong new growths. The older wood can be recognized because it is grey or black while new wood is pale brown. If you have trouble differentiating between the two, prune at harvest time next year, cutting out the branches carrying fruit as soon as the currants are ripe. Blackberries should also be pruned now, again removing the canes that carried fruit but retain the current season's canes. Tie in the canes that are to be retained to their supports. Damaged, spindly or weak growths should be removed.

KITCHEN GARDEN
HARVESTING AND DIGGING

Most varieties of apples ripening now are suitable for storing for a few weeks but some will keep until next spring, given the right conditions. In the vegetable garden digging continues as crops are cleared from the ground. If you do not yet have a vegetable plot, this is a good time to get started.

Harvest apples and pears

A few apple and pear varieties may need to be left until late fall, but the majority will have been picked by the end of this month. A number of apple varieties store well, and in some instances they will remain in good condition until late spring. "Arkansas Black," "Golden Delicious," "Gold Rush," and "McIntosh."

Choose unblemished specimens, wrap them individually in sheets of wax paper and store in a single layer in boxes in a cool garage, cellar or shed.

An alternative method is to place six apples in a strong plastic bag, punch a few holes in the bag with a pencil and tie the top loosely, leaving a small gap. This method is good for varieties that tend to shrivel. Pears do not store for very long though, and need inspecting daily because they must be eaten immediately they are ripe—they spoil within a day or two.

BELOW: **Apples are ripe and ready for picking once the stalk separates easily from the spur when the fruit is lifted gently.**

Clear vegetable crops

By now, crops such as pole and bush beans, summer cabbages, marrows and so on will be more or less finished, and the plants can be cleared away. Unless the spent crop plants are badly diseased, add them to the compost pile to rot down. Tough, woody stems, like those of some brassicas, are very slow to rot and can either be shredded before being added to the pile, or be burned instead. As rows of crop plants are removed, dig the soil over and add compost or manure as available.

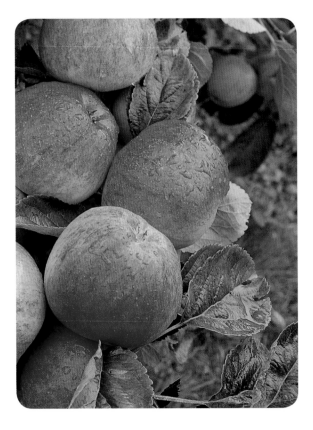

Start a new vegetable plot

Home-grown vegetables are always welcome, and are very rewarding to grow. While a few vegetables can always be grown in containers on the patio or among the flowers, a dedicated vegetable plot will give you a lot more scope for trying out new, exciting varieties. Make the plot as large as is practical for you to look after.

1 If the vegetable plot is to be made in the lawn, it will be necessary to strip off the turf. This can be done by cutting parallel strips in the grass with a half-moon edging iron, and undercutting the turf with a sharp spade (right). Hiring a turf cutter is worthwhile for large areas.

2 If the turf that has been removed is good quality, it can be relaid elsewhere, or perhaps sold. Otherwise, it can be stacked upside down to rot, when it will make an excellent loam for potting or for mixing with growing soil mixes.

3 The newly exposed soil should be well cultivated, either digging it by hand (left) or using a mechanical cultivator. Although the cultivator is quicker and easier, double digging allows deeper cultivation and gives better results in the long run—as long as you have the necessary time and stamina to do it. Spread the job over several weeks if necessary.

4 While digging, incorporate as much rotted garden compost or manure into the soil as possible; this improves fertility and soil structure, allowing heavy soils to drain more freely and light soils to become more moisture retentive. The plot should be left roughly dug over winter to allow frost to break down the clods into finer crumbs.

ABOVE: Wrapping apples separately before storing will help to prevent rot spreading if one of them starts to decay. Only unblemished fruits should be stored; damaged apples will not keep.

5 A soil testing kit is a worthwhile investment, giving you an idea of the acidity and nutrient levels in the soil (left). Acidity (pH) testing is usually quite accurate and will indicate whether an application of lime is necessary. Nutrient analysis is rather less reliable, but will still give a guide to your soil's fertility.

MID-FALL

117

LATE FALL

 Tidying up and preparing plants for the colder weather ahead continues, but planning for next season starts in earnest now, with new plantings to be made and seed orders to be filled out. This is a good time to have the lawn mower overhauled so that it's ready for next spring.

At this time of year we really notice how the days are shortening. For many gardeners, the only time the garden can be seen in daylight is at weekends, and all the tasks that need to be done have to be crammed into two short days, provided the weather allows. Fortunately there are few really pressing jobs.

It's important, though, that you protect the more tender plants before the coldest weather arrives. Night frosts will already have struck in many gardens, but the most damaging, sustained freezing temperatures are usually a feature of the winter. Don't forget to lag outdoor taps and water pipes, too.

Any damage to plants and garden structures caused by fall gales should be repaired quickly. Fences are particularly prone to problems, so check that fence posts and panels are sound. Garden sheds may also be showing signs of wear and tear. Secure roofing felt that has been loosened, and check for leaks inside, carrying out repairs as necessary. It is vital to have dry storage conditions available for many items including tools and machinery, fertilizers and chemicals, as well as produce such as tree fruit and root vegetables.

ABOVE: **The deep blues of** *Gentiana sino-ornata* **enrich the garden's color scheme.** OPPOSITE: *Viburnum tinus* **"Eve Price" offers a frothy interest to the fall garden.**

Weeds seem to keep growing whatever the weather, and weeding should be carried out as necessary. Since many chemical herbicides need weeds to make rapid growth to work most efficiently, hand weeding is generally the best approach in late fall and winter.

ORNAMENTAL GARDEN
GENERAL TASKS

If you want to repeat the display of bright, late summer and fall color from chrysanthemums, it's time to lift the roots and box them up for winter, ready to provide cuttings next spring. You don't have to wait until spring to take hardwood cuttings, though; they are easy to root and can be taken now.

Chrysanthemum roots

Some varieties of the so-called florists' chrysanthemum are hardy enough to overwinter in the garden, but the best quality plants are produced from cuttings taken in the spring. As the plants finish flowering now, they can be cut down to around 6in/15cm and the roots lifted carefully with a garden fork. Shake off some of the soil clinging to them, and box up the roots in almost-dry peat or potting compost.

Store the boxes of roots in a frost-free greenhouse or cold frame, garden shed, garage or similar place. In mid to late winter they will be brought into a heated greenhouse and watered in to start them into growth, but for now they should be kept virtually dry. If you grow a number of named varieties, tie a label around each stem to identify them.

RIGHT: **Lifting chrysanthemums: as the plants stop flowering at this point in the year, it is time to cut them down and lift their roots with a fork.**

Protecting alpines from rain

Low-growing alpines will often stand any amount of cold, but many will not tolerate wet weather in winter. Susceptible alpines can be protected by suspending a sheet of glass or clear plastic horizontally over the

plants, holding it in place by sliding it into notched wooden stakes, or laying it on top of bricks (weight it down to prevent the wind blowing it away). Free air circulation around the plants is vital.

Take shrub cuttings

Many garden shrubs can be propagated by hardwood cuttings that usually root easily and need very little care. A cold frame is an ideal place to overwinter the cuttings, but a sheltered position in the open garden will do as long as it has some protection from excessive rain. Some cuttings may be rooted by the following spring, but others may take 12 months or more before they are rooted sufficiently to be planted out in their growing positions.

1 Select strong, healthy growth which has been made in the current season. The shoots should be of around pencil thickness; thin, weak stems do not make good cuttings.

2 On deciduous shrubs, most leaves will have fallen, but any remaining can be brushed away (right). Cut the stems into 6in/15cm pieces, discarding the thinner tips. Make sure you know which is the top and bottom of each section.

3 With evergreen shrubs, remove the leaves from the lower two-thirds of the stem on each cutting. Dip the bases of the cuttings into hormone rooting powder or liquid (below), and insert them into pots of moist, sandy cuttings mix. Then you should place the pots in a cold frame or sheltered spot in the garden.

4 Shrubs that can be increased by this method include aucuba, buddleja, buxus (box), cydonia (quince), forsythia, philadelphus (mock orange), sambucus, spiraea, viburnum, and weigela. Climbers such as vitis (grapevine) and trees such as salix (willow) and populus (poplar) also grow well from cuttings.

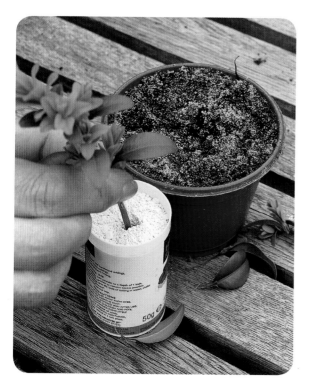

Tidy borders

Continue to tidy flower borders, cutting down dead stems and removing dead and dying foliage. If left, they provide handy overwintering sites for a range of garden pests, especially slugs and snails. These can cause an enormous amount of damage in the spring when they feast on the succulent new shoots that start pushing up through the ground.

LAWNS AND WATER GARDENS
GENERAL TASKS

Lawns now start to show signs of wear on heavily used routes as the soil becomes compacted in wet weather. The grass may need a final cut before the mower is sent away for servicing, ready for next spring. Garden ponds should need little attention unless the weather turns particularly cold.

ABOVE: **Aerating compacted areas of lawn is important to help surface water drain away. It is easily achieved with a garden fork.**

Aerating turf

When the soil is moist it is easily compacted. A frequently trodden route across the lawn will soon become muddy now, with its covering of grass gradually thinning and being worn away. Since it is important that air can reach the roots of the grass and that surface water can drain away at all times of the year, action should be taken as soon as worn patches are noticed. If the damage is not corrected, moss is likely to develop in place of the grass.

Try to redirect foot traffic away from the worn places if possible. Use a garden fork to spike the compacted areas, driving the prongs into the turf some 3–4in/7.5–10cm deep. Waggle the fork backward and forward gently to enlarge the holes slightly before removing it. Repeat over the whole area to leave the rows of holes evenly spaced in both directions.

Lawn mowers

If the grass has continued to grow, give it a final cut with the blades set high before sending the lawn mower away for its annual service. It is far better to get this done now than wait until next spring—that's when everyone else has the same idea, meaning you have to wait weeks before you get it back. Alternatively, service the mower at home if you have a basic knowledge of mechanics. After a season of grass cutting, the blades will need resharpening and adjusting so that they cut cleanly and do not tear the grass. Although this can also be carried out at home, it is not an easy job and is best done professionally.

Protect ponds from cold weather

If a garden pond freezes over for more than a couple of days, fish may be killed by the toxic gases trapped beneath the ice. The easiest way to prevent this is to install a pond heater.

1 At this time of year it is very important to keep the water free of any kind of decaying vegetation, whether this is dead leaves from water plants or fall leaves from nearby trees. Remove dead and dying leaves regularly, and cover the pool with a net to keep them out if necessary.

2 Remove the pond pump if one is installed, and clean and service it before storing it for the winter (right). If the pool is within reach of a power supply, install a pond heater. This keeps only a small area of the pond free of ice, but allows the air in and toxic gases to escape.

3 If it is not possible to use a pond heater, a ball floating on the surface of the water will delay freezing as it moves about in the wind (left). And if the water does freeze, boiling water poured around the edge of the ball enables it to be removed, leaving a hole in the ice. Hollow polystyrene packaging material can also be used.

4 Most sunken garden ponds are in no danger of freezing solid, but miniature ponds in half barrels are a different matter—they lack the insulation of the soil around them. In all but mild areas, fish from barrels should be moved under cover. Lagging the barrels with several layers of bubble wrap helps protect water plants.

Stop feeding fish

As the water temperature drops, fish become inactive and will not take food until the water warms up again in the spring. They live off stored body fat through the winter, so it is important to build them up in the early fall. Any food given from now on will sink to the bottom of the pool and rot, polluting the water.

LATE FALL

KITCHEN GARDEN
GENERAL TASKS

Harvesting the winter vegetable crops usually begins now, once the first few frosts have bitten; protection from hungry wild birds may be necessary, too. Although many gardeners find the whole subject of fruit pruning mystifying, it can be kept quite simple, and will ensure maximum crops.

Prune fruit trees

Apple and pear trees that are grown as open-centered bushes or small trees are not difficult to prune. The object is to maintain a well-shaped tree that carries as much fruiting wood as possible, while also bearing young branches to provide replacement fruiting wood in future seasons. Start by pruning out any dead, dying or diseased branches. Then remove crossing branches, and branches that are growing into the center of the tree. Now cut back strong-growing young laterals (side-shoots) by about half to two-thirds of the current season's growth, depending on how vigorous the growth is (the more vigorous the shoot, the more lightly it should be pruned because winter pruning stimulates growth). The tips of the leaders (main branches) should be pruned more lightly, cutting back the current season's growth by about one-quarter. Finally, remove some of the older branches which have borne fruit to encourage the production of new replacement shoots.

BELOW: **Long-arm pruners are very useful for reaching high fruit tree branches; you may be able to avoid using a stepladder.**

Lift root crops

Many root crops such as parsnips, rutabaga, maincrop carrots, salsify, and scorzonera are usually hardy enough to stay in the ground all winter, where they will keep in better condition than in store. However, if the weather becomes really cold and the soil freezes, it can be impossible to prise the crops from the icy ground. Lift a small supply now and store them in boxes of soil near the house so that they are easily accessible in cold weather. A few leeks can be stored alongside them because these are also difficult to harvest in freezing weather.

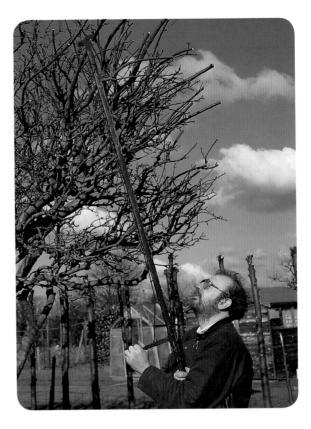

Keep birds at bay

A well-planned vegetable plot should contain a variety of vegetables that can be harvested through the winter, but wild creatures will be hungry too, and only too ready to take advantage of a free meal from your garden. Some form of deterrent is often necessary to obtain your share of the harvest.

1 Brassicas such as cabbages and Brussels sprouts provide invaluable winter fare, but the plants are prone to damage by pigeons. In a cold spell, a crop can be reduced to a skeleton of veins within hours, so choose some protection.

2 Bird scarers can help to deter pigeons though their effect is often disappointing (right). Moving, glittery or noisy objects are best. Strips of foil or unwanted CDs can be hung from canes to shine as they twist in the wind, while children's windmills on sticks provide noise and movement. Tautly stretched tape from old audio or video tapes makes a low hum in the breeze.

3 A physical barrier can be provided by stretching twine between stakes in a criss-cross fashion over the top of the crop, or using horticultural blanket draped over the tops of the plants. This needs to be secured at the edges to prevent it lifting up and being blown away (below).

4 Growing brassicas in a fruit cage is the most reliable answer where pigeons are a real problem. In cold regions, the netting over the top will need to be replaced with large mesh netting for the winter to prevent snow from collecting—its weight would weigh down and tear the net.

Brussels sprouts and parsnips

There is a saying that it is not worth harvesting Brussels sprouts and parsnips until they have had a good touch of frost to improve their flavor. Whether frost actually does improve the flavor is open to question, but it is certainly true that they are both hardy enough to withstand severe frosts without damage, allowing the harvest to be extended right through the winter.

KITCHEN GARDEN
PLANTING AND SOWING

An out-of-season treat of new potatoes may be available from specially treated seed potatoes planted in the summer; remember to order potatoes from the catalogs for more conventional planting in spring. Unlikely as it seems, it is also time for sowing some vegetables outdoors for next year.

Sowing beans and peas

As long as you sow the right varieties, both beans and peas will overwinter as seedlings to give early crops next year—you could be picking beans and peas by late spring.

Choose a reasonably sheltered site for sowing, on free-draining soil. On heavy soils there is a risk of the seeds rotting, and in this case it is better to sow them in pots or boxes in an unheated greenhouse for planting out in the spring. The crop will not be so early, but it will prove to be more reliable.

Sow beans 4–6in/10–15cm apart in rows 12in/30cm apart; peas are sown rather more closely in the row, at 2–3in/5–7.5cm apart. Depending on your climate zone and prevailing local conditions, your local garden center should be able to advise on the most appropriate varieties to sow in your garden or greenhouse.

BELOW: **Certain varieties of beans can be sown at this time of year to give a crop late the following spring.**

Summer-planted potatoes

Specially prepared, cold-stored seed potatoes that were planted in the summer produce a crop some two or three months after planting. Check them now, by scraping away some soil to expose the developing tubers. As long as most are large enough to eat they can be lifted when you want to use them. If the weather is mild, the tubers may continue to swell, but most will have finished developing by now. Do not lift the entire crop as you would for maincrop potatoes; they keep best if left in the soil up to midwinter, insulated from freezing weather with a mulch of straw or dry bracken.

Plant fruit trees and bushes

With the development of dwarfing rootstocks, it is possible for fruit trees such as apples and pears to be grown even in small gardens. Soft fruit bushes such as currants and gooseberries are also easy to grow and provide very welcome crops in the summer.

1 Choose from the wide variety of fruit trees available from specialist nurseries. The plants are often supplied bare root, by mail order, and should be planted as soon as possible after delivery. Most garden centers stock a reduced but reasonable selection, usually container grown.

2 Dig out a planting hole wide enough to take the roots of the tree without cramping, and deep enough for the tree to be planted at the same depth it was growing in the nursery. Fork over the soil in the base of the hole and add some well-rotted garden compost or planting mixture.

4 Return the excavated soil to the hole, gently jiggling the tree up and down while you do so in order to ensure that the soil sifts between the roots. Then you should tread the soil firm with the ball of your foot as you proceed (above).

5 When the hole is refilled, attach the tree to the stake with an adjustable tree tie (above). If container-grown, remove the root ball carefully having watered it well a few hours before, put it in the base of the hole and firm the soil around it.

3 Hammer the stake in position before planting the tree to avoid damaging the tree roots. A short stake is all that is necessary. Check that the size of the hole is correct for the tree, then spread the tree roots out in the base of the planting hole (above).

ABOVE: Cherry trees grow particularly well if they are trained against a reasonably sheltered wall or fence. Morello types are most popular.

FALL
TASKS & PLANT OVERVIEW

Early fall tasks

GENERAL
- Watch out for fungus diseases around the garden
- Deal with fallen leaves
- Clean and put away garden furniture

ORNAMENTAL GARDEN
- Plant spring bulbs
- Sow hardy annuals to overwinter
- Take cuttings of evergreens and plant hardy evergreen shrubs
- Move tender plants under cover before the frosts. Provide outdoor protection for slightly hardier ones
- Replace annuals and summer bedding with spring bedding
- Continue to clear containers and replant with bulbs and spring bedding
- Clear and weed around fall-flowering bulbs and perennials
- Prepare sites for fall planting of bare-root trees and shrubs
- Protect decorative berries from birds
- Take cuttings of old-fashioned and shrub roses
- Check ties and stakes on trees

LAWNS
- Sow new lawns
- Rake and aerate lawns, and give them an fall feed
- Repair bald patches, broken edges, bumps and dips

WATER GARDEN
- Net ponds against falling leaves
- Remove tender pond plants before the frosts

KITCHEN GARDEN
- Plant spring cabbage
- Harvest maincrop potatoes
- Support winter brassicas if needed
- Lift maincrop carrots and beets
- Thin out seedlings
- Pick outdoor tomatoes
- Harvest pumpkins and squashes before the first frosts
- Sow winter lettuce under a cloche or tunnel
- Plant onion sets for an early crop

Mid-fall tasks

GENERAL
- Remove fallen leaves and turn them into leaf mold
- Clear away all garden debris to avoid pests and diseases
- Protect vulnerable plants from rain and cold; beware of early frosts

ORNAMENTAL GARDEN
- Tidy herbaceous borders and divide border plants; apply bonemeal to borders and around shrubs and trees
- Plant tulips and hyacinths; plant lily bulbs as they become available
- Remove and burn diseased leaves fallen from roses
- Plant bare-root trees and shrubs
- Lift and store dahlia roots when the leaves have been blackened by frost
- Lift and store gladioli and tuberous begonias
- Finish planting spring bedding
- Protect newly planted shrubs from strong winds

LAWNS
- Continue to sweep up leaves and repair damaged areas of grass. Mow as necessary
- Apply bulky top-dressing
- Lay turf for new lawns

WATER GARDEN
- Remove submersible pumps from ponds; clean and store them
- Tidy pond plants and marginals, removing leaves from the water

KITCHEN GARDEN
- Continue harvesting crops, and store fruit and vegetables. Pick remaining apples and pears
- Remove vegetable plants as they finish cropping; begin digging and adding organic matter to soil
- Finish planting spring cabbages
- Take hardwood cuttings of soft fruit
- Plant new rhubarb crowns
- Prune blackcurrants, blackberries, and hybrid berries

Late fall tasks

GENERAL
- Note gaps in the borders and make plans to fill them
- Protect outdoor taps and water pipes from freezing
- Check bonfire piles for hibernating hedgehogs before lighting

ORNAMENTAL GARDEN
- Continue tidying borders. Leave top-growth for winter protection in cold areas. In exposed gardens, prune roses lightly to prevent root rock
- Continue planting bare-root trees and shrubs
- Take hardwood cuttings from shrubs
- Protect alpines from rain
- Lift chrysanthemums and box roots to provide cuttings in spring
- Finish planting tulips and hyacinths
- Continue to remove weeds
- Tidy alpines and rock gardens

LAWNS
- Give a last cut if necessary, then send mower for service and blade sharpening
- Aerate compacted areas
- Continue turfing in mild spells

WATER GARDEN
- Protect ponds and fish from cold. Stop feeding fish

KITCHEN GARDEN
- Sow beans and hardy peas for overwintering
- Continue digging spare ground
- Begin harvesting parsnips and Brussels sprouts. Lift some root crops for use in case the soil becomes frozen
- Check summer-planted, cold-stored potatoes and lift when ready. Order new seed potatoes from catalogs for the best choice of varieties
- Plant new fruit trees and bushes; begin winter pruning of fruit
- Continue weeding as necessary
- Protect winter brassicas from birds

Ornamental plants in season

Early fall

TREES AND SHRUBS

Caryopteris x *clandonensis*
Ceanothus (Californian lilac)
Clerodendrum bungei
 (glory flower), *C. trichotomum*
Erica (heath)
Hebe
Hydrangea macrophylla
Leycesteria formosa
 (Himalayan honeysuckle)
Malus (crab apple)
Perovskia atriplicifolia

Rosa (flowers and hips) (rose)
Vinca major (greater periwinkle),
 V. minor (lesser periwinkle)

PERENNIALS AND BEDDING PLANTS

Achillea (yarrow)
Aconitum napellus (aconite)
Anemone hybrida
Aster
Eryngium (sea holly)
Helenium
Hemerocallis (day lily)
Kniphofia (red hot poker)

Rudbeckia (coneflower)
Schizostylis coccinea (kaffir lily)
Sedum spectabile (ice plant)
Solidago (Aaron's rod)

BULBS

Amaryllis belladonna
Colchicum (fall crocus)
Crinum x *powellii*
Crocosmia crocosmiiflora
Crocus (fall-flowering species)
Cyclamen
Nerine bowdenii

ABOVE: **The daisy-like flowers of helenium.**

Mid-fall

TREES AND SHRUBS

Acer (maple)
Berberis (deciduous) (barberry)
Cercidiphyllum japonicum (katsura
 tree)
Cotoneaster
Erica (heath)
Euonymus alatus (winged spindle),
 E. europaeus and others
Fothergilla major
Hamamelis
Hippophae rhamnoides (sea
 buckthorn)
Hydrangea quercifolia
Malus (apple, crab apple)
Parthenocissus (Virginia creeper,
 Boston ivy)
Gaultheria mucronata

Pyracantha (firethorn)
Rosa (hips) (rose)
Skimmia
Sorbus
Vitis coignetiae, V. vinifera
 (grapevine)

PERENNIALS

Aconitum napellus (monkshood)
Anemone hybrida
Aster
Gentiana sino-ornata
Liriope muscari (lily turf)

Physalis alkekengi var.
 franchettii (Chinese lantern)
Sedum spectabile (iceplant)

BULBS

Amaryllis belladonna
Colchicum (common crocus)
Crinum x *powellii*
Cyclamen
Galanthus reginae-olgae
 (snowdrop)
Nerine bowdenii
Schizostylis coccinea (kaffir lily)

LEFT: *Schizostylis coccinea*, **the kaffir lily, is one of the latest-flowering border plants. The variety "Sunrise" has delicate shell-pink flowers.**

Late fall

TREES AND SHRUBS

Aucuba japonica (spotted laurel)
Berberis (barberry)

Callicarpa (beauty berry)
Clematis orientale, C. tangutica
Cornus alba (red-barked
 dogwood)
Cotoneaster
Fatsia japonica (japanese aralia)
Gaultheria mucronata
Jasminum nudiflorum (jasmine)
Leycesteria formosa (Himalayan
 honeysuckle)

LEFT: **Sunflowers provide bold, bright splashes of color and dramatic interest.**

Malus (apple, crab apple)
Prunus x *subhirtella* "Fallalis" (fall
 cherry)
Pyracantha (firethorn)
Rosa (hips) (rose)
Salix alba var. *vitellina*
 "Britzensis"
 (white willow)
Skimmia
Sorbus
Symphoricarpos (snowberry)
Vaccinium (bilberry)
Viburnum

PERENNIALS

Aster

Helianthus (sunflower)
Gentiana sino-ornata
Iris unguicularis
Liriope muscari (lily turf)

BULBS

Colchicum (fall crocus)
Crocus (fall-flowering species)
Cyclamen
Galanthus reginae-olgae
 (snowdrop)
Nerine bowdenii
Schizostylis coccinea
 (kaffir lily)
Sternbergia lutea (fall daffodil)

OVERVIEW

EARLY WINTER

The weather is often entirely unpredictable now. Penetrating frosts and icy winds; continuous dull, depressing rain; or mild, calm, sunny days more like early fall: anything is possible. It may not be the best time to be working outside, but seize your opportunities when they arise.

A greenhouse is a real boon for a keen gardener now—whatever the weather, you can get on with growing plants in comparative comfort. In contrast to the often bleak scene outdoors, the greenhouse can be full of color from bulbs and pot plants, and given there's enough heat, some seed sowing can begin.

Although the grass has stopped growing and the mower has been put away for the winter, that doesn't mean you can entirely ignore the lawn. This is the time of year when it is most likely to suffer wear and tear, so be prepared to act promptly in order to prevent damage from occurring.

Wild birds can be a nuisance at times, but most gardeners appreciate the life they bring to the garden in winter, and are happy to encourage them. The fall season with its fruit, seeds, berries, and insects is over, and it's time to start putting out food on the bird table. But remember, once you start feeding, you must keep it up because the birds will come to rely on you. Remember to provide water for drinking and bathing, too, particularly in freezing weather.

If the garden is looking dull, cheer it up by planting some containers of hardy winter plants like flowering

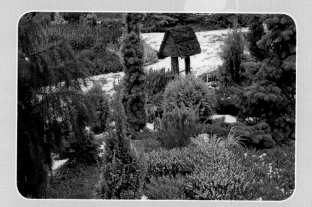

ABOVE: **Now is the time to tidy up your flower borders because any slugs and snails sheltering in weeds and debris will attack young shoots.** OPPOSITE: **The sweet-scented, pale yellow flowers of *Mahonia japonica* are carried all through the winter, undeterred by the coldest weather.**

Viola (pansies) and heathers, and variegated foliage plants. In the kitchen garden there will probably still be winter digging and fruit tree pruning to get on with, and don't forget to send off those seed orders before the spring rush.

EARLY WINTER
GENERAL TASKS

Encourage birds into the garden now by providing them with regular, easy meals, and they may stay around to keep down insect pests in the spring and summer. Take care of other animals too—the fish in ponds will be badly affected if the pond stays frozen over for more than a day or two.

Feeding garden birds

As soon as the weather turns cold, birds begin to find it increasingly difficult to obtain sufficient food. Not only are there fewer insects, berries, and fruit in the garden, but there are increasingly fewer daylight hours in which to eat. Supplying food regularly for birds can make all the difference to their survival, especially the smaller species.

Use a bird table placed in the open, and protected as far as possible from cats. A roof over the table helps to keep the food dry. Do not put out more food until the birds have cleared up what is there because excess food falls to the ground and attracts vermin. Suitable foods include peanuts, soaked brown breadcrumbs, apples and other fruit, suet and dripping, oatmeal, fresh (not desiccated) coconut, seeds, and so on. Special feeders are available for different foods and species of birds, including models that prevent the food being taken by squirrels.

BELOW: **Put out a supply of bird food regularly all through the winter months. Once birds start to visit a bird table, they will come to rely on it.**

Winter digging

Digging is best done a little at a time to avoid back strain, so continue steadily with the job over the next few weeks. Incorporate as much organic matter into the ground as possible while digging, especially on light or heavy soils. Garden compost, stable manure, spent mushroom compost, spent hops, and similar materials will all help to improve the texture of the soil, enabling light soils to retain more moisture and heavy soils to drain more freely. If you find digging too hard or time consuming, a mechanical cultivator can be used instead once a whole plot is cleared for cultivation.

Protect lawns from wear

Cold, wet conditions increase the likelihood of damage to turf as the soil is easily compacted and the grass is unable to make new recovery growth. A frequently walked route over the lawn—from the house to a garden gate or shed, for instance—will soon become obvious in winter, with the grass becoming thin and bare patches eventually appearing.

Encouraging alternative routes that do not cross the lawn is one solution, but the quickest, most straightforward route is always the one most likely to be used. If this route crosses the lawn it may be best to accept the situation and make a firm path. An informal stepping-stone path is often an appropriate style; it appears less intrusive than a solid path. A slightly curving route is good, but it should not deviate too much from the more direct pathway or it will not be used.

1 Ensure the stones are placed the correct distance apart to give an easy walking pace. Lay the first slab in place and cut around it with a half-moon edging iron (above, left). Undercut the turf with a spade to remove it; excavate the soil and replace with a 1in/25mm layer of sand.

2 Drop the slab into place; its surface should end up just below that of the surrounding grass so that mowing can take place over the top of it. Check the level and settle the slab into place by tapping firmly with the handle of a lump hammer or similar tool to bed the slab down (above, right).

Thawing holes in frozen ponds

If ponds remain frozen over for more than two days, thaw a hole in the ice to allow toxic gases to escape and prevent them from poisoning fish. Do not break the ice with a heavy object such as a hammer as fish may be harmed by shock waves traveling through the water. Instead, thaw a hole; fill an old tin can or pot with boiling water and stand it on the ice. It may need refilling several times if the ice is thick. If possible, use a pond heater to stop the pool freezing over again.

ORNAMENTAL GARDEN
GENERAL TASKS

It's a good time to clean up the walls behind deciduous climbers now that the leaves are off the plants; it's surprising how many pests lurk under the tangle of stems. And don't put containers away just because the summer bedding plants have finished—they can be enjoyed through the winter, too.

Containers for winter interest

Many gardeners rely heavily on plants in containers to provide color near the house, on the patio and around the garden during the summer, but far fewer make full use of them through the winter months. There are lots of plants that will give a good display in winter, even in the coldest weather—try dwarf evergreen shrubs (especially variegated varieties), dwarf conifers, winter-flowering viola (pansies) and heathers, ornamental cabbages, and trailing plants such as hedera (ivy).

Tubs, window boxes, and even hanging baskets in a sheltered position can be used. In very cold areas, insulate the roots of the plants by lining the inside of the container with bubble wrap before filling with soil mix. Bubble wrap can also be used to lag already-planted containers by being tied around the outside. Be careful with terracotta (clay) containers outdoors in the winter. Porous material absorbs water which expands when frozen, and this can shatter the pot; look for brands which are guaranteed frost proof.

Checking trees for root rock

Recently planted trees (and shrubs) can be disturbed by wind: it catches the branches and rocks the plants backward and forward. This disturbs the roots in the soil and often opens up a hole around the base of the stem; water may channel down and cause rot. Check trees and shrubs regularly; firm them back in the soil with the ball of your foot if necessary.

BELOW: **Make use of evergreens as well as winter-flowering subjects such as pansies and primulas to give containers winter and spring interest.**

Protecting young trees

Newly planted trees are often attacked by rabbits in gardens near fields or open spaces. Rabbits (and other small mammals) strip off the bark, weakening the tree and making it vulnerable to disease. If they remove a complete strip of bark from around the whole trunk, the tree will die. They can be thwarted, though, by using a rabbit guard in the form of a spiral plastic strip slipped around the trunk. Being spiral, the guard is able to expand as the trunk swells and does not restrict the tree's growth, even if forgotten.

Wall maintenance under climbing plants

The appearance of an area of blank wall is greatly improved by growing climbing plants over it, but maintenance work on the wall beneath the plants will be necessary occasionally to keep it in good condition. Now that the climbers are not in active growth, this is a good time of year to carry out such work.

1 Climbing plants should be grown on a trellis fixed to the wall rather than directly on the wall itself. It improves the air flow round the plants while making the wall accessible for maintenance. Attach the trellis to battens 2in/5cm thick and fix to the surface of the wall (right).

2 Prune back shoots that have outgrown the available space, and thin out the climber's growth if necessary. Unscrew the trellis and carefully lower it, still clothed with the climber's growth, to ground level. Two people are necessary to do this unless the trellis is very small.

3 The wall behind a dense climber is a favorite hiding place for snails, and you will probably find a surprising number clinging to the wall's surface. Remove and dispose of them, and then sweep all the dirt and debris away from the wall with a stiff broom or brush (left).

4 Carry out any necessary repairs to brick or plasterwork before re-attaching the trellis. If screws are difficult to work with, a hook and eye system can be used to attach the trellis instead. Great care is needed to avoid damage to the main stem of the climber while the trellis is being lowered and raised.

ABOVE: **This is the time of year for checking trees and shrubs for root rock; they may well have been disturbed by windy weather.**

Keeping hellebore flowers clean

The winter-flowering *Helleborus niger* (Christmas rose) bears its blooms very close to the ground, where they may be spoiled by soil splashes if it rains. When the plants are in bud, tuck some straw or similar material around their base to prevent this.

KITCHEN GARDEN
GENERAL TASKS

Continue pruning fruit trees during the dormant season, except when the weather is frosty. Winter digging of the vegetable plot should also be proceeding; it is worth digging the ground as deeply as you can, adding plenty of organic matter to improve the soil.

Protecting beans and peas

Pea and bean seeds sown in the vegetable plot earlier in the fall should have germinated and be showing through the soil by now. Although they are hardy, very cold and windy weather will take its toll of the young plants, so it is worth giving them a little extra protection to see them through the worst spells.

Plants can be protected by glass barn cloches placed over the rows that will keep off the worst of the cold weather and wind, and protect the plants from excess rain. The glass acts as a mini-greenhouse, trapping the warmth of any sun there may be. Unfortunately glass cloches are very prone to breakage, and can be dangerous, especially where there are children or pets in the garden. Mini-polytunnels are a safer option, although condensation can be a problem, causing fungal rots to affect the seedlings. One of the easiest materials to use is lightweight horticultural blanket that is draped loosely over the crop. The edges must be pegged down or secured to prevent the blanket from blowing away in windy weather.

LEFT: **Protect fall-sown beans and pea seedlings from the worst of the cold weather and wind with mini-polytunnels.**

Pruning large trees

Most modern fruit trees are grown on dwarfing or semi-dwarfing rootstocks, but older trees can grow very tall and wide-spreading, making pruning difficult. If you use a ladder it must be secure, so have someone hold it steady. Long-arm pruners make reaching high branches easier; make sure the blades are sharp and the cutting mechanism works smoothly.

Start winter digging

Since digging is satisfying but hard physical work, large plots should be completed in stages to avoid the back problems that trouble so many over-enthusiastic gardeners. Digging is best carried out as early in the winter as possible, leaving the ground rough for the maximum time to allow frosts to break up the clods of soil.

1 Dig a trench one spit (the depth of the spade's blade) deep across the top of the plot (above). Throw the soil into a wheelbarrow so that it can be moved to the other end of the plot. Try to keep your spine straight while digging.

2 Fork over or chop the soil at the base of the trench with the spade. Move backward and dig a second trench behind the first (above). Throw the soil from this to fill the trench in front. Try to turn the soil over as you throw it.

3 Continue in this way until you reach the other end of the plot. If you have any rotted manure or garden compost to incorporate, it should be placed at the base of each trench before it is filled in. Annual weeds can be buried, but perennial weed roots should be dug out and removed.

4 Once the last trench has been dug, fill it in with the soil from the first trench that has been barrowed to the end of the plot. Leave the soil surface rough; repeated freezing and thawing of the moisture in the soil over the winter will break down the clods and improve soil structure.

Pruning fruit trees

Continue pruning bush trees as described on page 124. Pruning in the dormant season stimulates strong, vigorous growth the following spring, and that is why the major pruning of trees trained as restricted forms takes place in summer. Hard winter pruning of apples and pears grown as cordons or espaliers would result in uncontrolled growth. Winter pruning on trained trees should mainly be restricted to removing dead, dying and diseased wood, and thinning out overcrowded spurs.

Plums should not be pruned in the winter because this invites an invasion by silver leaf disease spores. The disease slowly weakens the trees, and forms bracket fungi on affected branches that release spores mainly during the late fall and winter. The spores enter new wood through fresh wounds. Plums should be pruned in the spring and summer when spores are less likely to be around, and in any case the trees more quickly produce natural resins to seal over pruning cuts. The popular plum variety "Victoria" is particularly prone to this disease, which also affects almonds, apricots, and cherries, although not usually producing such serious effects as it does on plums.

MIDWINTER

 This is often the most trying season of the year for gardeners. The weather may be at its most miserable and, although the shortest day is just past, there is no real evidence yet of the daylight hours lengthening. Spring might seem a long way off but in reality there is not too long to wait.

All the dormant-season tasks in the garden continue. Planting bare-root specimens of new trees and shrubs will be possible for some weeks yet; if the weather is freezing or very wet when the plants arrive, heel them in until conditions improve. After heavy frosts, check plantings in case they need firming back into the soil if the frost has lifted them.

Evergreen plants continue to give good value, especially the variegated varieties that light up the garden in dull weather. Many of the trees and shrubs flowering now have the bonus of an intense fragrance, and more and more bulbs are blooming.

The prolonged wet spells show up any badly draining areas. If puddles are still standing on the soil surface hours after the rain has stopped, drainage needs to be improved.

This is the most likely time for snow. Snow can make the garden look beautiful, but if you can bring yourself to spoil its unsullied whiteness it's a good idea to take action to prevent it from damaging plants and trees. It's only the physical weight of the snow that does the damage; snow actually helps to insulate plants against the cold.

ABOVE: **Pyracantha, with its startling red berries, will liven up any garden at this time of year.**

Some border plants can be increased by root cuttings, and in the vegetable garden the soil can be made ready for early spring sowings. In the greenhouse things are moving ahead rapidly—stock up with the equipment you need for the busy sowing and growing season ahead.

MIDWINTER
GENERAL TASKS

Snow hides all the imperfections of the winter garden and covers it in a pristine whiteness, but it can bring problems for the gardener, especially if it persists for more than a few days. Frost is more common than snow in most areas, and brings its own set of difficulties, particularly for lawns.

Preventing snow damage

A moderate fall of snow can pose a real danger to evergreen trees and shrubs. In just a few hours they can be permanently misshapen, or branches can be broken by the weight of snow.

If the snowfall is heavy enough, knock it from the branches of any tree or shrub that looks as though it may be damaged. It is usually easily dislodged with a broom, but you will need to do this shortly after the snow has fallen—don't wait for it to freeze again otherwise it becomes much more difficult.

The thaw brings more problems, as a large amount of water is released as the snow melts. On lawns, look out for round patches of dying, yellow grass that gradually enlarge and may show signs of a fluffy white mold. This is snow mold, a fungus disease that is common on lawns that have been covered in snow for some time, especially if they have been walked over regularly. Treat the disease with a lawn fungicide.

Storing tools

Garden tools need to be kept in good condition if they are to give reliable service, and the winter is an ideal time to give them all a thorough overhaul. Hand tools such as spades and forks should be cleaned thoroughly after use, removing all soil, and the metal parts rubbed with an oily rag. Wooden handles can be smoothed down with sandpaper to prevent splinters.

The moving parts of tools such as shears and secateurs should be oiled, and blades of all cutting implements can be sharpened with a carborundum stone. Don't forget to sharpen the blades of tools such as hoes and edging irons as well. Any tools that are not being used over the winter should be stored in a dry place, and tools that have reached the end of their useful life should be replaced before the main growing season starts in readiness.

LEFT: **Snow may bring a seasonal beauty to the winter garden, but it can also spell problems for some trees and shrubs.**

Make a cold frame

Cold frames are more useful in the garden than is generally realized. They are invaluable for overwintering slightly tender or young plants, and are ideal for hardening off greenhouse plants destined for outdoors in the spring. While purpose-made aluminum and plastic cold frames can be bought, it is quite easy to make your own, often entirely from waste materials.

1 A typical cold frame has a wooden or brick base about 12–18in/30–45cm high at the back, sloping down toward the front, and is covered with a glass lid called a light. The usual size for a frame is around 4x2ft/120x60cm but size can be adjusted to suit your specific needs.

2 Demolition yards can often supply glazed window frames very cheaply, and they make excellent lights. Choose those with as large an area of glass as possible because glazing bars cut down the amount of light considerably. Once you have obtained the lights, build the base to fit.

3 If the frame is constructed in a sheltered area it is unnecessary to cement the bricks together. The window frames can be laid on top of the base and held in place by bricks around the edge (above). With wooden bases, attach the frames with hinges to make ventilation easier.

4 On cold days a piece of old carpet or sacking should be laid over the frame for extra protection (left); in sunny weather ventilate the frame by removing the light or propping it open with a wooden stay. In windy areas, make sure the open light is secure and cannot be blown away.

LEFT: **Walking over frosted grass will crush and kill the frozen stems, leaving a pattern of blackened footprints later on. Walking on the lawn in wet weather should also be avoided. Make an extra effort to stick to paths in winter.**

ORNAMENTAL GARDEN
GENERAL TASKS

Even though it is midwinter, there are definite signs of growth from spring-flowering bulbs. Help them on their way by making sure they are not smothered by weeds and debris. Meanwhile, root cuttings are an unusual but easy way of increasing a range of border plants, shrubs, and trees.

Bulbs in store

Many plants that develop specialized storage organs, such as bulbs, corms and tubers, can be stored over winter in a cool, dry, frost-free place such as a garden shed; if left in cold, wet soil in the garden there is often a real risk of them rotting away. However, they are not immune to rotting even when lifted and stored under cover.

There are several fungi and bacteria that are responsible for storage rots. Many of the pathogens are present in the soil while some are airborne, and they usually attack the plants through damaged tissue. Check stored bulbs regularly all through winter, and remove and destroy any that show signs of rotting. Rots may take the form of red, brown or black lesions that are often soft but may also be hard and dry; mold growth may also be visible. Dust remaining bulbs with a fungicide powder to try to prevent the spread of the problem.

BELOW: **Boxes of daffodil bulbs can be stored during the winter months provided their environment is dry and frost-free.**

Emerging spring bulbs

The leafy shoots of spring bulbs are already emerging through the soil. Carefully remove weeds, leaves and other plant debris from around the shoots, and prick over the soil between them with a hand fork if there is room; this helps to aerate the soil and prevents a soil "cap" from forming. Where bulbs are planted under trees, moss may form on the soil surface; this does not harm the bulbs but you may want to scrape away the moss to improve the general appearance. On poor soils, a balanced fertilizer can be sprinkled around the bulbs once the surface has been cleared.

Take root cuttings

Most gardeners are familiar with the idea of taking cuttings from shoots and encouraging them to form new roots. Less well known is the technique of growing new plants from sections of root which send out new shoots. This is an easy way to propagate plants, and one of the few methods of propagation which can be carried out in midwinter.

1 A number of shrubs and herbaceous plants can be grown from root cuttings taken in the dormant season; among them are anchusa, *Anemone x hybrida*, papaver (poppy), phlox, primula (primroses), romneya (tree poppy), daphne, and *Rhus typhina*.

2 The cuttings can be taken at any time in the dormant season when the soil is not waterlogged or frozen. Herbaceous plants can be lifted carefully, or the plants can be left in situ and the soil scraped away to expose some roots if lifting is not practical.

3 Choose firm, healthy roots, removing two or three from each plant by cutting them cleanly with a knife (above). Replace the soil around the parent plant and firm it in well. Trim off any whiskery side roots from the cuttings and place them in a plastic bag to prevent drying out.

4 Cut the prepared roots into sections about 2in/5cm long, but make sure you know which is the top and bottom of each piece. Insert into pots of moist, sandy cuttings mix so that their tops are level with the soil surface (above). Keep in a cold frame over winter.

Refirm specimens

A heavy frost can expand the soil and cause it to lift around the roots of newly planted trees and shrubs, loosening them in the ground. Inspect plants after a frost, and where necessary, firm them back in place by treading around them with the sole of your boot, pushing the soil back against the stems.

KITCHEN GARDEN
GENERAL TASKS

Plant canes and bushes to extend your range of soft fruits, and check to see if your vegetable garden would benefit from the addition of lime to the soil. Cloches help to get the soil ready for early sowings, but if you can't wait that long, grow your own salad in a jelly jar in a matter of days.

Adding lime to soil

Most plants grow best in soil that is just the acid side of neutral, but vegetables may benefit from the addition of lime that reduces the soil acidity. This is largely because club-root disease, which affects brassicas, is less severe in neutral or alkaline conditions. Lime should not be added unless a pH test has shown that it is necessary; if the pH is 6.5 or above, lime is not needed. It is certainly not necessary to lime the vegetable garden every year as was once a traditional practice.

Take a number of soil samples from different parts of the garden and use a proprietary soil-testing kit to give a reading (full instructions are on the pack). The most useful test is for soil acidity (pH) because some plants will grow well only in acid soils. Tests for major nutrients (nitrogen, phosphorus and potassium) can also be carried out, but the results are not always reliable.

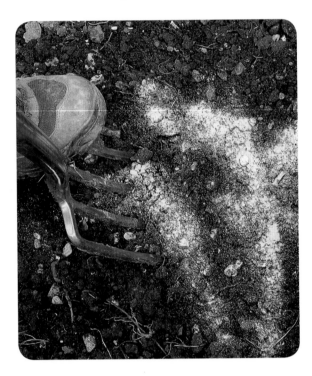

RIGHT: **Add lime to the soil only if a pH test shows that it is necessary. It may help to prevent club-root disease in the vegetable garden.**

Bushes, canes, and fruit trees

Fruit and vegetables form an important part of a healthy diet, and having plenty of home-grown fruit to harvest will certainly enable you to increase your consumption. Spells of good weather will allow you to plant fruit trees and soft fruit canes and bushes now.

Extend your range of soft fruits by trying some of the new, improved varieties that find their way into the catalogs every year. Particularly popular are the hybrid berries (mainly raspberry/blackberry crosses) such as boysenberry, silvanberry, tayberry, youngberry, sunberry, and veitchberry. They should provide a talking point and a good crop of tasty fruit.

Sprouting seeds for winter salads

Winter is a difficult time to produce fresh salad crops, but sprouting seeds couldn't be simpler to grow. They are ready in a matter of days, and have a pleasant crunchy texture and a range of interesting flavors. Many varieties are also thought to be beneficial to health, with particularly high concentrations of cancer-preventing compounds. A good range of suitable seeds for sprouting is available from the mail order catalogs of major seedsmen.

1 Sprouting seeds can be grown in a wide-necked glass jar topped with a piece of muslin or fine mesh net secured with an elastic band. A square cut from an old pair of nylon pantyhose makes a good cover.

2 Put a couple of spoonfuls of seeds into the jar and cover them with water; allow them to soak for a few hours or overnight (right). Drain the water off through the top of the jar, fill with fresh water, swirl around the jar and immediately drain the water off again.

3 Place the jar of seeds in a moderately warm position. If they are grown in the dark the sprouts will be white; if they are in the light they will be green and have a slightly different flavor. Every day, fill the jar with fresh water, swirl it round and immediately drain it away.

4 After a few days the sprouts are ready to eat (above); they will bulk up to almost fill the jar. Among seeds that can be grown are mung beans, alfalfa, and fenugreek; mixtures are also available. Only buy seeds produced for sprouting as many pulses are poisonous if eaten raw.

The vegetable plot

In a sheltered place in the vegetable garden, cover an area of ground with cloches to get it ready for seed sowing a little later. Although the cloches might help to trap what heat there is, this is not why they are useful. Their main purpose is to keep the rain off the soil so that it can dry out, enabling it to be broken down to the fine crumbs necessary to form a seedbed.

LATE WINTER

 Although the weather can be terrible, there is no longer any doubt that spring is on its way. The days are lengthening; buds on the branches of trees and shrubs begin to swell, and more and more early bulbs are producing their flowers. Get those dormant season tasks finished as soon as you can.

If jobs such as winter digging, planting bare-root trees and shrubs, and pruning fruit trees are not yet finished, this is the time to complete them. In most areas roses can safely be pruned now, too.

A few dry, breezy days will help to get the soil in good condition for sowing to take place outdoors shortly. If you do not know what type of soil you have in the garden, this is a good time to carry out tests to find out its composition.

Flower borders should be tidied, removing weeds and debris that shelter slugs and snails. This is particularly important because the tender young shoots of plants newly emerged through the soil are very vulnerable to these pests. Mulching is equally important because it helps prevent further weed growth, keeps some of the moisture in the soil ready for drier weather, and makes the garden look much tidier and more attractive.

In the kitchen garden, winter crops such as leeks and parsnips need to be used up before they start into growth again, and if you have forced rhubarb and kale for early crops you should harvest them now.

ABOVE: **Variegated evergreens like *Hedera colchica* "Sulphur Heart" are particularly valuable for brightening the garden in the winter months.** OPPOSITE: ***Mahonia aquifolium* "Smaragd" supplies rich shapes and textures to the garden.**

ORNAMENTAL GARDEN
GENERAL TASKS

The new shoots of herbaceous plants will soon be appearing through the soil in milder regions, and hardy annuals that were sown last fall need to be provided with supports. If you want long-flowering plants especially suitable for containers, it's time to start begonia tubers into growth.

Border plants and slugs

If the weather is mild, some of the early herbaceous border plants will be growing, and their tender, succulent shoots are an irresistible lure to slugs.

Destroy slug habitats by clearing weeds and debris from the border and the surrounding areas: remember that they can travel some distance from the shelter of hedge bottoms and similar hideouts. Protect individual plants by surrounding them with a barrier; crushed egg shells, sharp sand and grit, garden lime, and clinker are traditional deterrents, but strips of plastic are much more effective.

Cut strips about 3–4in/7.5–10cm wide from empty plastic bottles and push them firmly into the soil around each plant so that 2–3in/5–8cm remains above ground. At this time of year it's usually a better and more effective method of dealing with slugs than slug pellets.

If you have to use a slug killer, there are a number of organic controls available on the market that are less harmful to the wildlife than methiocarb and metaldehyde, including a biological control using a parasitic nematode.

RIGHT: **Slugs spend the day concealed in weedy areas or hedge bottoms, traveling surprising distances to feed during the night.**

Mulching flower borders

Remove weeds from flower borders and mulch the borders with, say, chipped bark or mushroom compost to deter fresh weed growth and improve the look of the bed. The mulch will also help to retain soil moisture throughout the spring and early summer. Be careful not to apply mulch too closely around emerging plants because it can encourage slugs (see above). Leave a clear space immediately around the crowns, as described, or mulch up to the plastic strip barriers.

Start begonia tubers

Tuberous-rooted begonias make excellent plants for pots and hanging baskets, and are not difficult to keep from year to year. Tubers that have been stored over winter can now be started into growth in a warm greenhouse.

1 Begonias produce rather odd-looking tubers which means it is not always easy to tell which is the top and which is the bottom (below). The top is dished, and shows signs of knobbly growth buds; the underside is rounded and whiskery, covered with fibrous roots.

2 Prepare a tray or pot of sandy, soilless cuttings compost and press the bases of the tubers into the surface (below). The concave side must face upward, and should not be covered with compost. Keep the tray in a light, warm position, ideally around 57°F/14°C.

3 Keep the soil mix moist, but take care not to splash water into the top of the tuber. If growth buds are slow to appear, lightly mist the tops of the tubers with a fine spray of water once, but otherwise keep the tops dry to avoid rotting.

4 Once strong growth buds appear, the plants can be propagated. Cut the tubers into two or three sections, each with a growth bud, or the buds can be allowed to develop into shoots which are used as softwood cuttings.

Hardy annuals

Hardy annuals that were sown last fall should be weeded and the plants thinned out if necessary. Provide them with supports to prevent them from flopping over as they grow. The most inconspicuous supports are twiggy sticks (such as peasticks) that can be cut from hedges or garden shrubs and pushed into the soil among the plants. As the annuals grow, they will hide these supports almost entirely. If your fall sowings did not survive the winter, don't worry—another sowing can be made next month.

KITCHEN GARDEN
GENERAL TASKS

Dry, breezy days at this time of year will dry out the soil and allow seedbeds to be prepared shortly, but if the weather should turn windy and cold, young crops may need some protection. Jerusalem artichokes are a very easy crop to grow, and the tubers can be planted now.

Protecting seedlings

This is still an unpredictable time of year as far as the weather goes—it can produce some of the coldest conditions of the winter, often after a mild spell has already started plants into growth. The young plants of beans and peas that were sown in the fall can be given a severe set-back by poor weather now, but they can be protected from the worst of it with cloches or lightweight horticultural blanket.

Spring cabbage plants not planted out in the fall can be set out in their cropping positions when the weather is suitable. Like the pea and bean seedlings, they can be protected with cloches or blanket if conditions deteriorate after planting.

BELOW **At this time of year it may be a good idea to use a horticultural blanket (or cloche) to protect pea and bean seedlings against harsh weather.**

Planting Jerusalem artichokes

Jerusalem artichokes are one of the easiest vegetables to grow—in fact you should take care where you plant them because they keep coming up year after year if any tubers are left in the ground. They are completely hardy, and grow in virtually any soil; the sunflower-like plants are very tall, so do not plant them where they will cast shade over other crops. The normal variety of Jerusalem artichoke has very knobbly tubers that can be difficult to prepare; "Fuseasu" is a smooth-skinned variety. Plant tubers 4in/10cm deep and 12in/30cm apart, with 3ft/90cm between the rows.

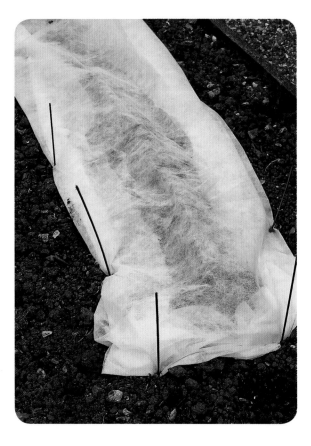

Prepare for pole beans

Pole beans are one of the most worthwhile crops for gardeners. They produce a very large crop in relation to the space they occupy, and have an extended season throughout the summer, right up until the first frosts. Although it is a little too early to think about raising the plants yet, it is not too soon to start preparing the soil where they are to grow.

1 Choose a warm, sheltered site for pole beans, preferably moving them to a new position each year to avoid root-rotting fungi building up in the soil. Dig a trench at least one spit deep—more if you can manage it—and 2ft/60cm or so wide. Fork over the soil in the bottom of the trench to break it up (right).

2 Beans need fertile, and above all moisture-retentive soil. Adequate levels of soil moisture are necessary to ensure reliable setting of the flowers (flowers often drop off unfertilized in dry conditions, leading to poor crops), and rapid development of tender, juicy pods.

3 Add a layer of moisture-retentive material to the base of the trench. Ideally this should be well-rotted manure containing plenty of straw (below), but a mix of materials such as grass clippings, spent hops, spent mushroom compost and even old newspapers can be used.

4 Leave the trench open to the rain until it is time for sowing or planting the beans after the last frosts in the spring. Then make sure the base of the trench is thoroughly soaked, by watering if necessary, before returning the topsoil and treading it thoroughly to firm.

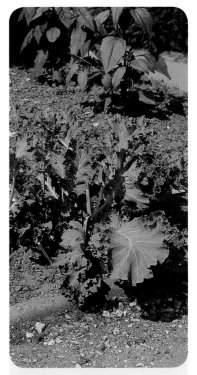

Kale and rhubarb

Stems of kale (pictured above) and rhubarb that have been forced into early growth in a frost-free greenhouse should be ready for cutting now. The shoots should have been kept completely dark by covering them with a black bucket or container– this gives the most tender results and prevents kale from becoming bitter.

Kale is an unusual luxury vegetable (not to be confused with kale beet, which is quite different). It is often compared to asparagus, but the creamy white stems have a flavor all of their own.

KITCHEN GARDEN
CROP ROTATION

It is not good practice to grow the same crops in the same places in the vegetable garden year after year. There are several reasons for this.

Different crops have slightly different nutrient requirements. Brassicas, for instance, are known as greedy crops (or gross feeders) because they take a high level of nutrients, particularly nitrogen, from the soil. If brassicas are grown on the same piece of ground year in, year out, the nutrients in the soil could soon be exhausted, particularly if no organic matter or fertilizers are added to replace them. Brassicas are also prone to certain specific pests and diseases, such as club-root; they can persist in the soil, or on crop remains, ready to infect the new crop the following year.

If a different crop is grown in the brassica's plot next year, however, it is likely to take different types of nutrients from the soil. It will also be immune to brassica-specific pests and diseases, so that the cycle of infection can be broken. This practice of ensuring that different types of crop are grown in succeeding years on the same piece of ground is known as crop rotation. Deciding exactly which crop should be grown where obviously needs careful planning. There are various crop rotation schemes, but a common one is to divide the types of crops that are grown into three main groups.

Dividing the crops

The first group is the brassicas—cabbages of all types, Brussels sprouts, kale, calabrese, cauliflower, and so on. They have a high nitrogen requirement, and are prone to club-root disease. The second group is root crops—

ABOVE **Peas tend to be placed in a group that includes lettuces and leeks, simply because they are neither root crops nor brassicas.**

LEFT **Cauliflowers fall into the brassicas group of vegetables. This group is known as "greedy crops" because they need a high level of soil nutrients.**

Crop rotation

	Bed A	Bed B	Bed C
Year 1	Brassicas	Roots	Peas & beans
Year 2	Peas & beans	Brassicas	Roots
Year 3	Roots	Peas & beans	Brassicas
Year 4	Brassicas	Roots	Peas & beans

Size matters

There is one major difficulty with a rotation, and that is the need for each of the three groups to occupy exactly the same amount of space. The imaginative use of miscellaneous crops (such as lettuce, marrows, spinach and so on) can help here because they can be placed in any of the three groups, as necessary, to balance things out. However, the rotation does not have to be followed slavishly—it will have to be adjusted for practical purposes.

ABOVE **Carrots belong to the root crop group, alongside potatoes, parsnips, beets, and Jerusalem artichokes.**

potatoes, parsnips, carrots, beets, Jerusalem artichokes, salsify, and scorzonera, and so on. They have a slightly lower nitrogen requirement, and are likely to be misshapen if fresh manure has been added to the soil recently. Finally there are peas and beans—these are unusual because they obtain nitrogen from the air rather than the soil, because of nitrogen-fixing bacteria that live on their roots. This means they will actually add to the amount of nitrogen in the soil.

Of course, not all crops fall neatly into one of these three groups. Crops such as rutabaga and turnips are both brassicas and root crops, so which group would they go in? And what about spinach, or marrows and zucchini, or onions? Rutabaga, turnips, and kohlrabi are included in the brassica group, mainly because they can be infected by club-root disease. Since spinach is a hungry crop with a high nitrogen requirement it also fits well into the brassica family.

Most other crops such as lettuces, tomatoes, marrows, leeks, onions and so on are generally included with the peas and beans, simply because they are neither brassicas nor true root crops. However, there are no hard and fast

rules about these miscellaneous crops, and onions are sometimes included with the root crops, while spinach joins the peas and beans, for example.

Establishing the rotation

The vegetable plot is divided into three and each of these three main groups of crops is grown in their own section—for example, brassicas in bed A, root crops in bed B and peas and beans in bed C. Next year, peas and beans move into bed A, brassicas into bed B, and roots into bed C. The following year they all move round one place again, and the year after that they are back where they started.

This means that the bed with roots can be manured at the end of the season ready for the brassicas, and the roots follow the peas and beans that have added nitrogen to the soil to make up for the absence of manure.

Four or five bed rotations are also possible by splitting the groups up further, but they become increasingly complicated. The three-bed scheme is the most practical for the majority of gardens.

WINTER
TASKS & PLANT OVERVIEW

Early Winter tasks

GENERAL
- Continue winter digging
- Make paths to avoid wear on lawns
- Cover compost piles to keep dry

ORNAMENTAL GARDEN
- Continue to plant containers for winter and spring interest
- Firm newly planted trees and shrubs after frosts
- Protect the blooms of *Helleborus niger* (Christmas rose) with straw on the ground
- Check trees and shrubs for root rock or lifting after frosts, refirming them if necessary
- Order flower seeds from catalogs, especially those needing an early start
- Put up tree guards to protect young trees against rabbits

LAWNS
- Avoid walking over frosted grass. Turfing is still possible if mild

WATER GARDENS
- Thaw holes in frozen ponds

KITCHEN GARDEN
- Protect fall-sown bean and pea seedlings
- Order seeds from catalogs
- Prune fruit trees

Midwinter tasks

GENERAL
- Check and maintain tools before putting them away for the winter
- Improve drainage where necessary

ORNAMENTAL GARDEN
- Knock snow off evergreens before their branches break
- Weed and check emerging spring bulbs outdoors
- Take root cuttings of phlox, papaver (poppy), verbascum (mullein), and other border plants
- Continue planting bare-root and container-grown trees and shrubs, and refirm newly planted specimens after frost.
- Heel in bare-root plants when weather is unsuitable for planting
- Order young plants from seed catalogs for delivery in early to mid-spring

LAWNS
- Keep off the grass in frosty or wet weather
- Watch out for snow mold disease
- Sweep away leaves and debris

KITCHEN GARDEN
- Force outdoor rhubarb for an early crop
- Sow sprouting seeds for winter salads
- Sow beans and peas for an early crop
- Order vegetable seeds, seed potatoes, young vegetable plants, and onion sets from catalogs as soon as possible
- Continue to check fruit and vegetables in store
- Cover the ground with cloches to dry it out ready for early sowings
- Continue to plant fruit trees, and soft fruit bushes and canes
- Complete pruning of fruit trees
- Deter birds from attacking fruit buds

LEFT: **Bulbs of narcissus "Paperwhite" planted now should be in flower in about six weeks**

Late Winter tasks

GENERAL
- Check tools and equipment, and buy new replacements if needed
- Carry out soil tests on various sites around the garden

ORNAMENTAL GARDEN
- Weed and clear borders, and mulch with bark
- Prune roses
- Finish planting bare-root trees and shrubs
- Weed overwintered hardy annuals and provide supports as necessary
- Protect vulnerable plants from slugs
- Sow *Lathyrus odoratus* (sweet peas) outside
- Prune winter jasmine after flowering
- Prune summer-flowering clematis hybrids
- Feed flowering shrubs with sulfate of potash

LAWNS
- Mow the grass lightly if necessary. Carry out repairs to edges and aerate compacted areas

KITCHEN GARDEN
- Use up winter vegetables such as leeks and parsnips from the garden before they regrow
- Complete winter digging and apply lime if necessary
- Prepare seed beds
- Use horticultural blanket, cloches etc. to protect pea and bean seedlings, and spring greens
- Set seed potatoes to chit (sprout) in a light place as soon as they are purchased
- Plant shallots and Jerusalem artichokes
- Prepare a pole bean trench with moisture-retaining compost
- Harvest forced kale and rhubarb as soon as the shoots are large enough
- Prune fall-fruiting raspberries
- Feed fruit trees and bushes with high-potash fertilizer

Ornamental plants in season

Early winter

TREES AND SHRUBS

Acer, especially A. capillipes, A. davidii, A. griseum (maple)

Arbutus unedo (strawberry tree)

Aucuba japonica "Crotonifolia" and others (spotted laurel)

Betula, especially B. ermanii, B. nigra (black birch), B. papyrifera (paper birch), B. utilis var. jacquemontii (Himalayan Birch)

Chimonanthus praecox (wintersweet)

Cornus alba (red-barked dogwood)

Corylus avellana "Contorta" (corkscrew hazel)

Cotoneaster

Elaeagnus x ebbingei

Erica carnea (alpine heath)

Euonymus fortunei, E. japonicus (variegated)

Fraxinus excelsior "Jaspidea" (common ash)

Hamamelis mollis (Chinese witch hazel)

Hedera (ivy)

Ilex (berry-bearing and variegated varieties) (holly)

Jasminum nudiflorum (jasmine)

Lonicera fragrantissima, L. standishii (shrubby honeysuckle)

Mahonia

Prunus serrula, P. x subhirtella "Fallalis" (fall cherry)

Pyracantha (firethorn)

Salix alba, S. babylonica var. pekinensis "Tortuosa" (willow)

Skimmia japonica

Sorbus

Tilia platyphylos "Rubra" (red-twigged lime)

Viburnum

PERENNIALS

Helleborus niger (Christmas rose)

Iris unguicularis

Schizostylis coccinea (kaffir lily)

RIGHT: **Snowdrops are among the earliest flowers of the year. The double flowers of** *Galanthus nivalis* **"Flore Pleno" are especially attractive.**

BULBS

Crocus imperati

Cyclamen coum

Galanthus (snowdrop)

Midwinter

TREES AND SHRUBS

Acer (bark effects) (maple)

Aucuba japonica (spotted laurel)

Betula (birch)

Camellia

Chimonanthus praecox (wintersweet)

Cornus alba (red-barked dogwood)

Corylus avellana "Contorta" (corkscrew hazel)

Cotoneaster

Daphne odora

Erica carnea (alpine heath)

Euonymus fortunei, E. japonicus (variegated varieties) (spindle tree)

Garrya elliptica

Hamamelis mollis (witch hazel)

Hedera colchica "Dentata Variegata" and others (ivy)

Hippophae rhamnoides (sea buckthorn)

Ilex (berry-bearing and variegated varieties) (holly)

Jasminum nudiflorum (jasmine)

Lonicera fragrantissima, L.

standishii (honeysuckle)

Mahonia

Prunus serrula, P. x subhirtella "Fallalis" (fall cherry)

Pyracantha (firethorn)

Salix alba (white willow), S. babylonica pekinensis "Tortuosa"

Skimmia japonica

Sorbus

Viburnum

PERENNIALS

Ajuga reptans (bugle)

Bergenia

Helleborus atrorubens, H. foetidus (stinking hellebore)

H. niger (Christmas rose)

Iris unguicularis

Phormium tenax (New Zealand flax)

Viola (winter-flowering pansies)

BULBS

Crocus ancyrensis, C. imperati, C. laevigatus, C. tomasinianus

Eranthis (winter aconite)

Galanthus (snowdrop)

Iris danfordiae, I. histrioides, I. reticulata

Late winter

TREES AND SHRUBS

Acacia dealbata (acacia)

Camellia

Chaenomeles japonica (Japanese quince)

Chimonanthus praecox (wintersweet)

Cornus alba (red-barked dogwood), C. mas (cornelian cherry)

Daphne odora, D. mezereum

Erica carnea

Garrya elliptica

Hamamelis (witch hazel)

Hedera colchica "Dentata Variegata"

Jasminum nudiflorum (winter jasmine)

LEFT: *Hamamelis intermedia* **"Westerstede" (witch hazel) bears its fragrant, ragged-petalled flowers on leafless branches.**

Lonicera fragrantissima, L. standishii (shrubby honeysuckle)

Magnolia campbellii

Mahonia x media "Charity" and others

Prunus incisa "February Pink" (Fuji cherry), P. mume (Japanese apricot) and others

Pyracantha (firethorn)

Salix alba (white willow), S. babylonica var. pekinensis "Tortuosa"

Sarcococca hookeriana, S. humilis (Christmas box)

Skimmia

Sorbus

Stachyurus praecox

Viburnum

PERENNIALS

Bergenia

Helleborus niger (Christmas rose), H. orientalis (Lenten rose)

Phormium tenax (New Zealand flax)

Primula (primrose)

Pulmonaria (lungwort)

Viola odorata (English violet)

BULBS

Anemone blanda

Chionodoxa (glory of the snow)

Crocus

Cyclamen coum

Eranthis hyemalis (winter aconite)

Galanthus (snowdrop)

Iris danfordiae, I. histrioides, I. reticulata

Narcissus (daffodil)

GLOSSARY

acid
referring to soil having a pH of less than 7, suitable for lime-hating plants

adventitious roots
roots springing directly from the plant stem

alkaline
referring to soil having a pH greater than 7, unsuitable for lime-hating plants

alpine
plants that naturally occur in mountainous regions above the tree line. Generally alpine is also used to refer to low-growing rock garden plants

annuals
plants that germinate, flower, produce seed, and die in one season

aquatic
plants that grow in water

bare root
plants that are lifted from the open ground for transplanting in the dormant season

bedding
plants that are set out in beds or containers to give a temporary, seasonal display of flowers or foliage

biological control
the deliberate use of a natural organism to control a pest or disease

blossom-end rot
a disorder where tomatoes and related plants bear fruit with a sunken, dark brown patch at the base. It is caused by a lack of calcium in the tissues as the fruit develops, generally because of water shortage

brassica
a member of the cabbage family, including vegetables such as Brussels sprouts, cauliflowers, turnips and so on

bulb
storage organ formed from a modified stem and leaf bases

cloche
low protective structure made from glass or plastic, used to protect plants from adverse weather. A floating cloche is a lightweight film of perforated plastic or fiber lying loosely on top of the crop

cold frame
an unheated, protective structure, usually with solid sides and a removable glass or plastic lid

compost
the organic substance produced by rotting down vegetative matter that is used as a soil improver or top-dressing. Can be bought commercially as well as homemade

RIGHT: **Bare-rooted conifers (here wrapped in hessian for transportation) are best transplanted during the dormant season.**

cordon
plant trained usually as a single stem with pruning to remove side-shoots (e.g. tomatoes and apples)

corm
a plant storage organ consisting of a swollen stem base. Unlike a bulb, a corm replaces itself each year

cuttings
portions of plants that are detached and encouraged to grow new roots or shoots (or both) in order to make new plants. Cuttings may be taken from stems, leaves or roots

deciduous
a plant which loses its leaves at the end of the growing season

dormant
plants, seeds and so on, that are temporarily not in active growth

drill
a shallow trench in the soil where seeds are sown; usually made with a draw hoe

dwarfing
rootstocks that control the growth of varieties which are grafted on to them, making them smaller and more compact than they would be if they were growing on their own roots.

earthing up
drawing soil up around the stems of plants. This may be to blanch them (e.g. leeks and celery), encourage the growth of tubers (e.g. potatoes) or simply to help support them in the ground (e.g. tall brassicas)

espalier
a trained form of fruit tree with horizontal tiers of branches

evergreen
a plant that keeps its leaves the whole year round (see deciduous)

force
to encourage a plant into early growth, usually by providing extra warmth. Light is often also excluded from plants being forced

fungicide
a chemical used to control fungus diseases

hardening off
the process of gradually acclimatizing plants raised under protection to outside conditions

hardy
able to survive the natural climate, including frosts, without protection. Half-hardy means able to survive outdoors for part of the year, but unable to withstand frost

herbaceous
a plant whose non-woody top-growth dies down to a rootstock in the dormant season

humus
the organic remains of rotted-down vegetable matter that improves soil structure and content

hybrid
a cross between two distinct parents. Crosses are often between plant varieties; they may also be between species (interspecific hybrids) or less often between genera (intergeneric or bigeneric hybrids).

insecticides
chemicals used to kill insects

laterals
a side-shoot growing from the main stem of a plant. A sublateral is a side-shoot growing from a lateral

leader
the terminal shoot of a plant or stem

leaf axil
the area where the leaf stem joins the plant stem, from which growth buds often arise

leaf mold
rotted down leaves used as a soil additive

RIGHT: **Firm strawberries well when planting, and make sure the soil remains moist.**

macro-nutrients
the minerals required by plants in relatively large quantities, including nitrogen, phosphorus, potassium, calcium, magnesium, and sulfur

micro-nutrients
minerals required by plants in very small quantities, such as iron, molybdenum, manganese. They are also known as trace elements

mulch
material applied in a layer to the soil surface. It may be organic (e.g. compost, shredded bark) or non-organic (e.g. gravel, plastic sheeting). Mulch retains soil moisture and inhibits weed growth

organic
derived from material that has once lived (i.e. plant or animal remains)

oxygenators
submerged pond plants that produce oxygen to keep the water clear and healthy

perennial
surviving for a number of years

pesticide
chemical used to control garden pests including insects, slugs and snails, mites and so on

photosynthesis
the process by which plants manufacture energy from light

pollination
transfer of pollen from the male to female parts of a flower

potting on
moving a plant into a larger container

pricking off
moving a seedling from the tray or pot in which it germinated to a container where it is given more room to develop

rotation
the moving of vegetable crops to different areas of soil each year to prevent the build up of pests and diseases

runner
a long stem which bears young plants at the end, or at intervals along its length

semi-ripe
shoots that have just begun to harden at their base but are not completely woody

softwood
shoots that are still soft and flexible, and show no signs of woodiness

soil mix
the medium used for growing plants in containers instead of garden soil. Various mixes are available for seeds, cuttings, and mature plants

tender
vulnerable to damage by cold temperatures, especially frost

tilth
soil which has been broken down to small, even crumbs, suitable for seed sowing

top-dressing
fertilizer or organic matter applied to the soil surface; also mulches such as gravel around alpine plants

tuber
a storage organ which consists of a swollen stem or root

variegated
marked with two or more colors. Usually applied to leaves, but can also describe stems and flowers

INDEX

A

acacia 106,155

acanthus 91, 108

acer 18, 49, 94

achillea 108–9

acid 154

aeration 84, 122, 142

African blue lily 106

agapanthus 106

allium 108

alpines 13, 26, 120

alyssum 15, 72

anchusa 143

anemone 143

annuals 13, 154

   hardy 38, 148–9

   sowing 15

apple

   harvesting 88, 116–7

   planting 127

   protecting 62, 144

   pruning 89, 124, 137

aquatics 44–5

arugula 64

Aster novi-belgii 79

astilbe 91

aucuba 121

azalea 58

B

barberry 38, 94

basil 76

bean 22, 46, 47

   crop rotation 152–3

   protection 136

   sowing 34, 46, 126

   staking 20

bear's breeches 89, 106

bedding plants 83, 134

   planting 40, 57, 111

   planting out 56–7

   replacing 96

beets 34, 47, 64

   crop rotation 153

lifting 101

begonia 109, 148–9

bell flower 109

berberis 28, 95

bergenia 51

berries 28, 94

betula 17

birch 17

birds 48–9, 94, 125, 132, 144

blackberry 144

blackcurrant 115

blanching 154

blossom 21, 28

blossom-end rot 156

bolting 64

bonemeal 96, 108–9, 111

border plants 16, 82, 121

   dividing 109

   mulching 13, 55, 148

   staking 14, 38, 68

bourbons 18

box 121

brassicas 64, 116, 152

   crop rotation 152–3

   protection 62, 125

   supporting 100

briza 108

broccoli 34, 100

broom 58

Brussels sprout 34, 64 101, 125, 152

buddleja 19, 121

bulbs 12, 56, 83, 142, 156

   naturalizing 97

   planting 26–7, 71, 111

   storing 112

bullrush 108

Bush bean 46,116

Buxus 121

C

cabbage 34, 87, 103, 116

crop rotation 152–3

planting 64

protection 125

sowing 22

storing 88

watering 46

cabbage palm 106

calabrese 34, 152

calendula 15

campanula 109

canes 144

capsicum 65

carlina 108

carrot 22, 34, 47, 64

   crop rotation 152–3

   lifting 101, 124

cauliflower 22, 34, 152

ceanothus 28, 58

Centaurea cyanus 15

cherry 127, 137, 144

choisya 28

Christmas rose 135

chrysanthemum 81, 120

clarkia 15

climbers 55, 121, 134–5

cloches 137, 145, 150, 156

   club-root 152–3

colchicum 71, 97

cold frames 103, 141, 156

compost 107, 156

conifers 16

containers 72, 134

   planting 40–1

   preparation 13

   protection 95

   replanting 82–3

   vegetables 47

cordons 156

cordyline 106

corms 109, 142, 156

corn 64

cornflower 15

Cornus alba 19

Cotinus coggygria 19

crab apple 16

crocus 83, 97, 111

currant 49, 115, 127, 144

cutting back 124

cuttings 156

   evergreens 95

   hardwood 115

   pinks 54

   potting up 81

   semi-ripe 71

   shrubs 120–1

cydonia 121

cynara 108

cytisus 58

D

daffodil 56, 97, 142

dahlia 40, 81

   lifting 109

   staking 70

   storing 109

damasks 18

daphne 143

dead-heading 12, 58, 72

deciduous 28, 95, 121, 156

deutzia 58

disbudding 70

diseases 152

   fruit 48

   kitchen garden 62

   potato blight 74

   rose 30

division 109

dormancy 156

drainage 13, 117, 122, 132

dwarfing 156

E

earthing up 156

earwigs 70, 81

echinops 109

eggplant 47

elder 19

Elodea canadensis 45

eryngium 108

erysimum 96

escallonia 19, 28

espaliers 156

eucalyptus 19, 106

evergreens 28, 110, 156

   cuttings 95

   planting 16–7, 29, 96

F

fall crocus 97

fences 80

fertilizers 108

fescue 108

festuca 108

floribunda 18

flowering cherry 16

footprinting 60

forcing 157

forsythia 121

Fritillaria meleagris 97

frost 106, 109

fruit 75, 115, 117

   diseases 62

   harvesting 88, 116

   maggots 48

   pests 30, 48–9, 62

   protection 21, 49, 62, 125, 144

   pruning 89

fruit trees

   blossom 21

   planting 127

   pruning 124, 136–7

   rootstocks 127, 136

fuchsia 81

fungicides 30, 62, 74

G

galanthus 27, 83

gallicas 18

genera 8–9

globe thistle 109

gooseberry 62
gooseberry mildew 62
grape hyacinth 97
grapevine 121
ground cherry 108

H
half–hardy annuals 106
hamamelis 94
hanging baskets 13, 41, 72
hardening off 141, 155
hardwood cuttings 115, 121
hardy 155
    annuals 15, 149
    evergreens 96
harvesting 88
    apple 116
    herbs 76
    pea 63
    pear 116
    pumpkin 100
    rhubarb 20
heathers 83, 134
hedera 83, 134
hedges 28, 59
hellebore 135
herbaceous borders 157
    mulching 55, 148
    planting 16
    slugs 148
herbicides 31, 134
herbs 76
holly 28, 108
honesty 108
hosta 109
humus 157
hybrids 8, 157
    tea rose 18
hydrangea 108

I
ilex 28, 94
invasive plants 157
iris 56, 108
ivy 83, 134

J
Japanese onions 86

Jerusalem artichoke 150, 153

K
kale 20, 34, 64, 100, 151, 154
kerria 58
kohlrabi 34, 47, 64, 155

L
lagging 123
laterals 89, 124, 157
lawns 123, 141
    bulbs 97
    mowing 33, 60, 122
    protection 32, 133
    sowing 85, 99
    turf 113
layering shrubs 39
leaders 157
leaf axil 70, 89
leaf mold 157
leek 21
    planting out 64, 77
    sowing 22, 34
lettuce 102
    crop rotation 152–3
    sowing 22, 34, 103
lighting 67, 70
lilac 58
limnanthes 15
Linnaeus 8–9
love-in-a-mist 108

M
Madonna lily 70–1
magnolia 39
malus 16
maple 16, 95
marigold 15, 40, 57
marrow 22, 88, 116, 155
Mexican orange blossom 28
mint 82
mock orange 58, 126
moles 60
moths 48, 62
mulching 31, 157
    alpines 13

borders 13, 55, 148
myosotis 96

N
narcissus 56, 111
naturalizing 97
nematodes 30, 38, 148
nemophila 15
nigella 108
non-hardy perennials 81
nymphaea 44–5, 84
nyssa 94

O
onion 88
    crop rotation 153
    Japanese 86
    planting 35, 102
organic material 157
osmanthus 28
overwintering 81, 141
oxygenators 112, 157

P
pansy 40, 83, 96, 130, 134
papaver 108–9, 133
parsnip 21, 22, 114, 124–5, 153
parthenocissus 94
passiflora 106
passion flower 106
pathogens 142
pea 46
    crop rotation 152–3
    harvesting 63
    protection 136, 144, 150
    sowing 34, 126
    staking 20
pear 116, 124
pelargonium 81
pepper 47, 65
perennials 16, 108, 157
    overwintering 81
pesticides 62, 157
pests 30, 38, 48, 60, 81
    fruit 48, 62
philadelphus 58, 121
phlox 143
phygelius 106

physalis 108
pinks 54
pipings 54
Pistia stratioides 98
plant names 8–9
planting
    alpines 26
    aquatics 45
    bedding 57
    bulbs 27, 97, 111
    containers 40–1, 47
    evergreens 16–7, 29, 96
    fruit trees 127
    herbaceous plants 16
    Jerusalem artichoke 150
    leeks 77
    onions 35, 102
    peppers 65
    potatoes 23
    rhubarb 114
    shrubs 16–7
    strawberry 87
    trees 16–7
    tulip 111
    winter crops 64
plum 137, 144
poached egg plant 15
pole bean 22
    preparing 151
    sowing 46
pollination 157
polytunnels 48, 136
ponds 42, 44–5, 84, 98
    making 43
    protection 123
    submersible pumps 112
    thawing 133
poplar 121
poppy 108, 143
populus 121
potato
    blight 74
    crop rotation 152–3
    earthing up 63
    lifting 101, 126
    planting 23
    protecting 101
potentilla 19
potting on 157

pricking off 157
primrose 96, 143
primula 96, 134, 143
propagation 39, 75, 143
protection
    alpines 120
    bean 136
    cabbage 125
    fruit 21, 49, 62,125, 144
    lawns 32, 133
    non-hardy plants 95
    pea 136, 144, 150
    ponds 123
    potato 101
    seedlings 150
    shrubs 95, 110, 140
    slugs 30, 49, 148
    trees 21, 134, 140
pruning
    fruit 89
    roses 18
    shrubs 19, 58
    trees 18, 124, 136–7
    wisteria 73
prunus 17, 28
pumpkin 88, 100

Q
quaking grass 108
quince 121

R
raddichio 64
radish 34, 47, 64, 102
rhododendron 39, 58
rhubarb 20, 114, 151
Rhus typhina 143
romneya 143
root crops 114
    lifting 101, 124
    rotation 152–3
root cuttings 20, 143
root rock 96, 110, 134–5
rooting runners 74
rootstock 95, 127, 136, 157
rose 18, 30, 68
rotation 157

rots 142
runners 75, 87, 157
rutabaga 64, 124, 154

S
salads 103, 145
Salix 121
salsify 34, 114, 124, 153
sambucus 19, 121
scabious 108
scallion 34
scilla 97
scorzonera 34, 124, 153
screens 28, 80
sea holly 108
Sedum spectabile 108
seedlings 86
 bean 46
 leeks 77
 protection 150
 sweet pea 14
 thinning out 39, 102
shallot 88
shrubs
 bare-root 110
 cuttings 71
 layering 39
 planting 16–7, 29, 82–3, 96
 protection 95, 110, 140
 pruning 19, 58
 root rock 134

skimmia 83
slugs 30, 49, 148
smoke bush 19
snails 28, 80
snakeshead fritillary 97
snowdrop 27, 83
softwood 157
soil mix 41, 47, 54, 71, 72, 82, 117, 157
sowing
 bean 126
 hardy annuals 15
 lawns 85, 99
 lettuce 22, 34, 103
 pea 34, 126
 preparation 22
 successional crops 34, 64
 spinach 22, 64, 86
 sweet pea 14
 vegetables 22–3, 34
spinach 34, 46
 rotation 153
 sowing 22, 64, 86
 thinning out 102
sprouting seeds 145
squash 100
squill 97
staking
 bean 20
 border plants 14, 38, 68
 dahlia 70
 pea 20

storing 88, 116–7
 bulbs 142
 dahlia 109
 herbs 76
 root vegetables 101
 tools 140
strawberry
 beds 74
 planting 87
 protection 49
 runners 75
successional crops 34, 64
support
 border plants 14, 38, 54, 68
 brassicas 100
 climbers 55, 135
sweet pea 14
Swiss chard 22, 34
syringa 58

T
tender 157
thinning out 102, 137
tie in border plants 54
toadstools 99
tomato 47, 75
top-dressing 113, 157
training
 climbers 55
 tomato 75
Trapa natans 98

tree poppy 143
trees
 bare-rooted 110
 planting 16–7, 127
 protection 21, 134, 140
 pruning 18, 124, 136–7
 root rock 134–5
 rootstocks 127, 136
trimming hedges 59
tubers 149–50, 135
tubs 13, 41, 72, 134
tulepo 94
tulip 96, 111
tunnels 48, 103, 136
turf 113
turnip 34, 64, 102, 113
typha 108

V
variegated plants 135
vegetables
 clearing 116
 containers 47
 harvesting 88, 100, 126
 lifting 101
 plots 117
 protection 101, 125, 150
 rotation 152–3
 sowing 22, 34, 46, 126
 watering 46
verbascum 106
viburnum 58, 121

vine weevils 38
Viola 40, 83, 96, 130, 134
Virginia creeper 94
vitis 121

W
wallflower 96, 111
water chestnut 98
water hawthorn 44–5
water hyacinth 98
water lily 45
watering
 containers 72
 hanging baskets 72
 lawns 60
 vegetables 46
wattle 106
weedkillers 31, 32
weigela 58, 121
willow 121
windbreaks 28, 80
window boxes 13, 41, 72, 83
wisteria 73
witch hazel 94

Y
yarrow 108–9
yucca 106

Y
zucchini 22, 47, 153

Acknowledgments

The publishers would like to thank Liz Eddison for photography and picture research, Coral Mula for illustration, Roger Benjamin, Georgina Steeds, and Smith's Nurseries, New Denham, Middlesex, for their help with properties; and the following for their help with images:

Aughton Green Landscapes–Tatton Park 2001, 85(b); James Basson–Hampton Court 2000, 82;
David Brun–Hampton Park 2000, 40; Bill Cartlidge–Tatton Park 2000, 7(tl); Paul Dyer–Chelsea 2001, 84;
Guy Farthing–Hampton Court 2000, 6, 17(bl); Sally Fell–Hampton Court 2001, 16, 96; David Gibson–Tatton Park 2001, 27(b);
Colin Luckett–Tatton Park 2001, 80; Ian Taylor–Chelsea 2001, 69br; Geoffrey Whiten–Chelsea 2001, 63(b).
Neil Holmes: 8(bl), 9, 119(t), 129(m), 131(t), 140; Harry Smith: 21, 48, 49, 62, 86, 94, 99(bl), 116, 124, 125(br), 133(b), 141(b), 144, 151(tr)